JN448653

NIV개정

지혜의 성경
영어 잠언
따라쓰기 1

이　　름 : ____________________

시작한 날 : ____________________

끝마친 날 : ____________________

또 어려서부터 성경을 알았나니 성경은 능히 너로 하여금 그리스도 예수 안에 있는 믿음으로 말미암아 구원에 이르는 지혜가 있게 하느니라
모든 성경은 하나님의 감동으로 된 것으로 교훈과 책망과 바르게 함과 의로 교육하기에 유익하니 이는 하나님의 사람으로 온전하게 하며 모든 선한 일을 행할 능력을 갖추게 하려 함이라

디모데후서 3장 15-17절

잠언의 소개

잠언은 '속담' 또는 '격언'이라는 뜻이며, 기록연대는 솔로몬의 재위기간인 B.C. 970-930년경으로 추정됩니다. 저자는 솔로몬(1:1), 아굴(30:1), 르무엘의 어머니(31:1), 지혜 있는 자(22:17)까지 포함하여 4명입니다.

잠언은 하나님의 백성이 갖추어야 할 지혜의 근본 내용과 옳고 그름을 판단하는 지혜의 본질에 대한 규명과 삶의 현장에서의 하나님의 백성으로 살아가는 구체적인 사례가 기록되어 있습니다.

영어 잠언 따라 쓰기의 특징

1. 영어 성경이 없어도 영어 성경을 읽고 쓰는 것이 즐겁습니다.
2. 영어 성경을 쓰면서 삶의 지혜가 자라납니다.
3. 영어 성경을 쓰면서 하나님의 자녀로 바르게 자라납니다.
4. 영어 성경을 쓰면서 옳고 그른 것을 판단하는 기준이 생겨납니다.
5. 영어 성경을 쓰면서 순종적인 자녀로 성장하게 됩니다.
6. 영어 성경을 쓰면서 좋은 글씨체를 갖게 됩니다.
7. 각 페이지마다 숙어와 예문, 각 장의 단어 뜻풀이를 통해 영어 해석에 도움이 됩니다.
8. 부록에 수록된 원어민 발음과 한글개역개정을 통해 영어 잠언이 쉽게 읽어집니다.

말씀을 따라 쓰기 전에 알아 두세요.

1. 말씀을 쓰기 전 성령님의 도움으로 영어 성경을 깨닫게 해 달라고 기도해 보세요.
2. 쓰면서 큰 소리로 따라 읽으세요. 암송의 효과를 얻을 수 있어요.
3. 모르는 단어는 함께 수록되어 있는 뜻을 찾아보세요.
   영어 성경을 쉽게 이해하게 해 줄 거예요.
4. 쓴 만큼의 날짜를 꼭 적어 보세요.
   얼마나 규칙적으로 영어 성경쓰기를 했는지 알 수 있습니다.
5. 영어 성경을 쓰고 난 후 부모님이나 선생님께 보여드려 검사를 받으세요.
   부모님과 선생님은 어린이에게 하고 싶은 말이나 축복의 문구를 써 주시면
   큰 힘이 됩니다.

Proverbs 1장 1~33절

1 The proverbs of Solomon son of
David, king of Israel:
2 for gaining wisdom and instruction;
for understanding words of insight;
3 for receiving instruction in prudent
behavior, doing what is right and
just and fair;
4 for giving prudence to those who
are simple, knowledge and discre-
tion to the young—
5 let the wise listen and add to their
learning, and let the discerning get
guidance—
6 for understanding proverbs and

add to …에 더하다[보태다]
Add to this she is also very intelligent. 여기에 더해서 그녀는 매우 영리하다.

parables, the sayings and riddles of
the wise.
7 The fear of the LORD is the beginn-
ing of knowledge, but fools de-
spise wisdom and instruction.
8 Listen, my son, to your father's ins-
truction and do not forsake your
mother's teaching.
9 They are a garland to grace your
head and a chain to adorn your neck.
10 My son, if sinful men entice you, do
not give in to them.
11 If they say, "Come along with us;
let's lie in wait for innocent blood,
let's ambush some harmless soul;
12 let's swallow them alive, like the

do not forsake 버리지 말라
Do not forsake me. 저를 버리지 마십시오.

grave, and whole, like those who go
down to the pit;
13 we will get all sorts of valuable
things and fill our houses with plun-
der;
14 cast lots with us; we will all share the
loot"—
15 my son, do not go along with them,
do not set foot on their paths;
16 for their feet rush into evil, they
are swift to shed blood.
17 How useless to spread a net where
every bird can see it!
18 These men lie in wait for their
own blood; they ambush only them-
selves!

lie in wait for …을 잠복하여 기다리다
Don't you see she lies in wait for you? 그녀가 숨어서 너를 기다리는 게 보이지 않니?

19 Such are the paths of all who go
after ill-gotten gain; it takes away
the life of those who get it.
20 Out in the open wisdom calls aloud,
she raises her voice in the public
square;
21 on top of the wall she cries out,
at the city gate she makes her speech:
22 "How long will you who are simple
love your simple ways? How long
will mockers delight in mockery and
fools hate knowledge?
23 Repent at my rebuke! Then I will
pour out my thoughts to you, I will
make known to you my teachings.
24 But since you refuse to listen when

take away 제거하다
Who will take away those empty bottles? 누가 저 빈 병을 치울 거야?

I call and no one pays attention when
I stretch out my hand,
25 since you disregard all my advice
and do not accept my rebuke,
26 I in turn will laugh when disaster
strikes you; I will mock when
calamity overtakes you—
27 when calamity overtakes you like a
storm, when disaster sweeps over
you like a whirlwind, when distress
and trouble overwhelm you.
28 Then they will call to me but I will
not answer; they will look for me
but will not find me,
29 since they hated knowledge and did
not choose to fear the LORD.

sweep over (감정 등이)[사람]을 압도하다
The song swept over my soul. 그 노래는 내 영혼을 압도했다.

30 Since they would not accept my
advice and spurned my rebuke,
31 they will eat the fruit of their ways
and be filled with the fruit of their
schemes.
32 For the waywardness of the simp-
le will kill them, and the compla-
cency of fools will destroy them;
33 but whoever listens to me will live in
safety and be at ease, without fear
of harm."

Proverbs 2장 1~22절

1 My son, if you accept my words and
store up my commands within you,

be at ease 안심하다, 마음 놓다
Just be at ease with yourself. 그냥 너 스스로를 편하게 만들어라.

2 turning your ear to wisdom and app-
lying your heart to understanding–
3 indeed, if you call out for insight and
cry aloud for understanding,
4 and if you look for it as for silver and
search for it as for hidden treasure,
5 then you will understand the fear of
the LORD and find the knowledge
of God.
6 For the LORD gives wisdom; from his
mouth come knowledge and under-
standing.
7 He holds success in store for the upr-
ight, he is a shield to those whose
walk is blameless,
8 for he guards the course of the

in store for …을 위해서 비축하여, 준비하여
We have some surprises in store for you. 너를 놀래 줄 일이 있다.

just and protects the way of his faith-
ful ones.
9 Then you will understand what is
right and just and fair—every good
path.
10 For wisdom will enter your heart,
and knowledge will be pleasant to
your soul.
11 Discretion will protect you, and un-
derstanding will guard you.
12 Wisdom will save you from the ways
of wicked men, from men whose
words are perverse,
13 who have left the straight paths to
walk in dark ways,
14 who delight in doing wrong and

save from …에서 구하다
Exercise can also save you from illness. 또한 운동을 하면 질병을 예방할 수 있다.

rejoice in the perverseness of evil,
15 whose paths are crooked and who
are devious in their ways.
16 Wisdom will save you also from the
adulterous woman, from the way-
ward woman with her seductive
words,
17 who has left the partner of her
youth and ignored the covenant
she made before God.
18 Surely her house leads down to
death and her paths to the spirits
of the dead.
19 None who go to her return or
attain the paths of life.
20 Thus you will walk in the ways of

lead down to …로 이끌다
The meadows lead down to the river. 풀밭은 아래로 강까지 이어져 있다.

the good and keep to the paths of
the righteous.
21 For the upright will live in the land,
and the blameless will remain in it;
22 but the wicked will be cut off from
the land, and the unfaithful will be
torn from it.

Proverbs 3장 1~35절

1 My son, do not forget my teaching,
but keep my commands in your
heart,
2 for they will prolong your life many
years and bring you peace and pros-
perity.

cut off from …에서 고립시키다
They felt cut off from the outside world. 그들은 외부 세계와 단절된 기분이었다.

3 Let love and faithfulness never leave
you; bind them around your neck,
write them on the tablet of your
heart.
4 Then you will win favor and a good
name in the sight of God and man.
5 Trust in the LORD with all your heart
and lean not on your own under-
standing;
6 in all your ways submit to him, and
he will make your paths straight.
7 Do not be wise in your own eyes;
fear the LORD and shun evil.
8 This will bring health to your body
and nourishment to your bones.
9 Honor the LORD with your wealth,

in the sight of …가 보기에는[…의 의견으로는]
We are all equal in the sight of God. 하나님의 눈에는 우리 모두가 평등하다.

with the firstfruits of all your crops;
10 then your barns will be filled to
overflowing, and your vats will brim
over with new wine.
11 My son, do not despise the LORD's
discipline, and do not resent his re-
buke,
12 because the LORD disciplines those
he loves, as a father the son he
delights in.
13 Blessed are those who find wisdom,
those who gain understanding,
14 for she is more profitable than
silver and yields better returns than
gold.
15 She is more precious than rubies;

brim over with …으로 차 넘치다
Her heart was brimming over with happiness. 그녀의 가슴에서는 행복감이 넘쳐흘렀다.

nothing you desire can compare
with her.
16 Long life is in her right hand; in her
left hand are riches and honor.
17 Her ways are pleasant ways, and all
her paths are peace.
18 She is a tree of life to those who
take hold of her; those who hold
her fast will be blessed.
19 By wisdom the LORD laid the earth's
foundations, by understanding he
set the heavens in place;
20 by his knowledge the watery
depths were divided, and the clouds
let drop the dew.
21 My son, do not let wisdom and

in place 제자리에 (있는)
Your advice was quite in place. 너의 충고는 아주 적절했다.

understanding out of your sight,
preserve sound judgment and dis-
cretion;
22 they will be life for you, an ornam-
ent to grace your neck.
23 Then you will go on your way in
safety, and your foot will not stum-
ble.
24 When you lie down, you will not be
afraid; when you lie down, your sleep
will be sweet.
25 Have no fear of sudden disaster or
of the ruin that overtakes the
wicked,
26 for the LORD will be at your side and
will keep your foot from being snared.

lie down (자거나 쉬려고) 눕다[누워 있다]
Go and lie down for a while. 가서 좀 누워 있어.

27 Do not withhold good from those
to whom it is due, when it is in
your power to act.
28 Do not say to your neighbor, "Come
back tomorrow and I'll give it to
you"–when you already have it
with you.
29 Do not plot harm against your
neighbor, who lives trustfully near
you.
30 Do not accuse anyone for no reason
–when they have done you no harm.
31 Do not envy the violent or choose
any of their ways.
32 For the LORD detests the perverse
but takes the upright into his confi-

plot against …에 반대하여 음모를 꾀하다
There's a plot against your father. 당신의 아버지를 반대하는 음모가 있어요.

dence.

33 The LORD's curse is on the house of
the wicked, but he blesses the
home of the righteous.

34 He mocks proud mockers but
shows favor to the humble and
oppressed.

35 The wise inherit honor, but fools get
only shame.

Proverbs 4장 1~27절

1 Listen, my sons, to a father's instr-
uction; pay attention and gain un-
derstanding.

2 I give you sound learning, so do not

pay attention 관심을 갖다
He often doesn't pay attention. 종종 그는 집중을 안 해요.

forsake my teaching.
3 For I too was a son to my father, still
tender, and cherished by my mother.
4 Then he taught me, and he said to
me, "Take hold of my words with all
your heart; keep my commands,
and you will live.
5 Get wisdom, get understanding; do
not forget my words or turn away
from them.
6 Do not forsake wisdom, and she
will protect you; love her, and she
will watch over you.
7 The beginning of wisdom is this: Get
wisdom. Though it cost all you have,
get understanding.

watch over …을 지키다
I used to watch over you. 내가 너를 지켜보곤 했다.

8 Cherish her, and she will exalt you;
embrace her, and she will honor you.
9 She will give you a garland to grace
your head and present you with a
glorious crown."
10 Listen, my son, accept what I say,
and the years of your life will be many.
11 I instruct you in the way of wisdom
and lead you along straight paths.
12 When you walk, your steps will not
be hampered; when you run, you
will not stumble.
13 Hold on to instruction, do not let it
go; guard it well, for it is your life.
14 Do not set foot on the path of the
wicked or walk in the way of evildo-

hold on to …에 매달리다, 의지하다
If you hold on to your dream, you can do it! 꿈을 잃지 않으면 이룰 수 있어요!

ers.
15 Avoid it, do not travel on it; turn
from it and go on your way.
16 For they cannot rest until they do
evil; they are robbed of sleep till
they make someone stumble.
17 They eat the bread of wickedness
and drink the wine of violence.
18 The path of the righteous is like the
morning sun, shining ever brighter
till the full light of day.
19 But the way of the wicked is like
deep darkness; they do not know
what makes them stumble.
20 My son, pay attention to what I say;
turn your ear to my words.

be robbed of 강탈당하다
I was robbed of my purse. 나는 지갑을 털렸다.

21 Do not let them out of your sight,
keep them within your heart;
22 for they are life to those who find
them and health to one's whole
body.
23 Above all else, guard your heart, for
everything you do flows from it.
24 Keep your mouth free of perversity;
keep corrupt talk far from your lips.
25 Let your eyes look straight ahead;
fix your gaze directly before you.
26 Give careful thought to the paths
for your feet and be steadfast in all
your ways.
27 Do not turn to the right or the left;
keep your foot from evil.

above all (else) 특히, 무엇보다도
Love is, above all else, the gift of oneself. 사랑은 무엇보다도 자신을 위한 선물이다.

Proverbs 5장 1~23절

1 My son, pay attention to my wisdom,
turn your ear to my words of insight,
2 that you may maintain discretion
and your lips may preserve knowl-
edge.
3 For the lips of the adulterous woman
drip honey, and her speech is
smoother than oil;
4 but in the end she is bitter as gall,
sharp as a double-edged sword.
5 Her feet go down to death; her steps
lead straight to the grave.
6 She gives no thought to the way of
life; her paths wander aimlessly, but

in the end 마침내
Real ability will win in the end. 결국에 가서는 실력이 승리한다.

she does not know it.
7 Now then, my sons, listen to me; do
not turn aside from what I say.
8 Keep to a path far from her, do not
go near the door of her house,
9 lest you lose your honor to others
and your dignity to one who is cruel,
10 lest strangers feast on your wealth
and your toil enrich the house of an-
other.
11 At the end of your life you will
groan, when your flesh and body
are spent.
12 You will say, "How I hated discipline!
How my heart spurned correction!
13 I would not obey my teachers or turn

keep from …하지 못하게 하다
I could hardly keep from tears. 나는 눈물을 참을 수 없었다.

my ear to my instructors.
14 And I was soon in serious trouble
in the assembly of God's people."
15 Drink water from your own cistern,
running water from your own well.
16 Should your springs overflow in the
streets, your streams of water in the
public squares?
17 Let them be yours alone, never to be
shared with strangers.
18 May your fountain be blessed, and
may you rejoice in the wife of your
youth.
19 A loving doe, a graceful deer–may
her breasts satisfy you always, may
you ever be intoxicated with her

share with …와 나누어 갖다
It cannot be shared with another body. 이것은 다른 신체와 공유될 수 없다.

love.
20 Why, my son, be intoxicated with
another man's wife? Why embrace
the bosom of a wayward woman?
21 For your ways are in full view of the
LORD, and he examines all your
paths.
22 The evil deeds of the wicked ens-
nare them; the cords of their sins
hold them fast.
23 For lack of discipline they will die, led
astray by their own great folly.

Proverbs 6장 1~35절

1 My son, if you have put up security

be intoxicated with …에 도취하다
He is intoxicated with his own power. 그는 자신의 권력에 도취되어 있다.

for your neighbor, if you have
shaken hands in pledge for a stranger,
2 you have been trapped by what you
said, ensnared by the words of your
mouth.
3 So do this, my son, to free yourself,
since you have fallen into your
neighbor's hands: Go–to the point
of exhaustion–and give your neigh-
bor no rest!
4 Allow no sleep to your eyes, no
slumber to your eyelids.
5 Free yourself, like a gazelle from the
hand of the hunter, like a bird from
the snare of the fowler.
6 Go to the ant, you sluggard; cons-

be trapped 함정에 빠지다
The train was trapped underground by a fire. 화재로 인해 기차가 지하에 갇혔다.

ider its ways and be wise!
7 It has no commander, no overseer
or ruler,
8 yet it stores its provisions in summer
and gathers its food at harvest.
9 How long will you lie there, you
sluggard? When will you get up
from your sleep?
10 A little sleep, a little slumber, a little
folding of the hands to rest–
11 and poverty will come on you like a
thief and scarcity like an armed man.
12 A troublemaker and a villain, who
goes about with a corrupt mouth,
13 who winks maliciously with his eye,
signals with his feet and motions

go about …에 착수하다
Just go about your business. 맡은 네 일이나 열심히 해.

with his fingers,
14 who plots evil with deceit in his
heart—he always stirs up conflict.
15 Therefore disaster will overtake him
in an instant; he will suddenly be
destroyed—without remedy.
16 There are six things the LORD hates,
seven that are detestable to him:
17 haughty eyes, a lying tongue, hands
that shed innocent blood,
18 a heart that devises wicked schemes,
feet that are quick to rush into evil,
19 a false witness who pours out lies
and a person who stirs up conflict in
the community.
20 My son, keep your father's command

rush into 급하게[무모하게] …하다
I don't want to rush into it. 나는 그것을 서둘러서 하고 싶지는 않아.

and do not forsake your mother's
teaching.
21 Bind them always on your heart; fasten
them around your neck.
22 When you walk, they will guide you;
when you sleep, they will watch
over you; when you awake, they will
speak to you.
23 For this command is a lamp, this
teaching is a light, and correction
and instruction are the way to life,
24 keeping you from your neighbor's
wife, from the smooth talk of a
wayward woman.
25 Do not lust in your heart after her
beauty or let her captivate you with

lust after 욕정[욕망]을 느끼다
She lusts after wealth and power. 그녀는 부와 권력을 갈망한다.

her eyes.
26 For a prostitute can be had for a loaf
of bread, but another man's wife
preys on your very life.
27 Can a man scoop fire into his lap
without his clothes being burned?
28 Can a man walk on hot coals
without his feet being scorched?
29 So is he who sleeps with another
man's wife; no one who touches her
will go unpunished.
30 People do not despise a thief if he
steals to satisfy his hunger when
he is starving.
31 Yet if he is caught, he must pay
sevenfold, though it costs him all

prey on …을 먹이로 하다
They do not prey on each other. 그들은 서로 약탈하지 않는다.

the wealth of his house.
32 But a man who commits adultery
has no sense; whoever does so
destroys himself.
33 Blows and disgrace are his lot, and
his shame will never be wiped away.
34 For jealousy arouses a husband's
fury, and he will show no mercy
when he takes revenge.
35 He will not accept any compensat-
ion; he will refuse a bribe, however
great it is.

Proverbs 7장 1~27절

1 My son, keep my words and store

have no sense 눈치가 없다
They have no sense of hygiene. 그들은 위생 관념이 없다.

up my commands within you.
2 Keep my commands and you will
live; guard my teachings as the
apple of your eye.
3 Bind them on your fingers; write them
on the tablet of your heart.
4 Say to wisdom, "You are my sister,"
and to insight, "You are my relative."
5 They will keep you from the adulter-
ous woman, from the wayward
woman with her seductive words.
6 At the window of my house I looked
down through the lattice.
7 I saw among the simple, I noticed
among the young men, a youth
who had no sense.

look down 내려다보다, 아래를 보다
The king looked down on his slave. 왕은 자신의 노예를 내려다보았다.

8 He was going down the street
near her corner, walking along in
the direction of her house
9 at twilight, as the day was fading,
as the dark of night set in.
10 Then out came a woman to meet
him, dressed like a prostitute and
with crafty intent.
11 (She is unruly and defiant, her feet
never stay at home;
12 now in the street, now in the
squares, at every corner she lurks.)
13 She took hold of him and kissed
him and with a brazen face she said:
14 "Today I fulfilled my vows, and I
have food from my fellowship offer-

take hold of …을 잡다, 쥐다
He took hold of his class. 그는 그의 반을 장악했다.

ing at home.
15 So I came out to meet you; I
looked for you and have found you!
16 I have covered my bed with colored
linens from Egypt.
17 I have perfumed my bed with myrrh,
aloes and cinnamon.
18 Come, let's drink deeply of love till
morning; let's enjoy ourselves with
love!
19 My husband is not at home; he has
gone on a long journey.
20 He took his purse filled with money
and will not be home till full moon."
21 With persuasive words she led him
astray; she seduced him with her

lead astray 미혹시키다, 타락시키다
Don't lead anyone astray. 다른 사람들을 나쁜 길로 인도하지 마라.

smooth talk.
22 All at once he followed her like an
ox going to the slaughter, like a
deer stepping into a noose
23 till an arrow pierces his liver, like a
bird darting into a snare, little
knowing it will cost him his life.
24 Now then, my sons, listen to me;
pay attention to what I say.
25 Do not let your heart turn to her
ways or stray into her paths.
26 Many are the victims she has brought
down; her slain are a mighty throng.
27 Her house is a highway to the grave,
leading down to the chambers of
death.

bring down 내리다, 떨어뜨리다
I need something to bring down the fever. 열을 내릴 만한 약을 좀 주세요.

Proverbs 8장 1~36절

1 Does not wisdom call out? Does not
understanding raise her voice?
2 At the highest point along the way,
where the paths meet, she takes
her stand;
3 beside the gate leading into the city,
at the entrance, she cries aloud:
4 "To you, O people, I call out; I raise
my voice to all mankind.
5 You who are simple, gain prudence;
you who are foolish, set your hearts
on it.
6 Listen, for I have trustworthy things
to say; I open my lips to speak what

lead into [이야기 · 연극 등]을 시작하다
The man is leading a class into the hall. 남자가 학급을 홀 안으로 안내하고 있다.

is right.
7 My mouth speaks what is true, for
my lips detest wickedness.
8 All the words of my mouth are just;
none of them is crooked or perverse.
9 To the discerning all of them are
right; they are upright to those who
have found knowledge.
10 Choose my instruction instead of
silver, knowledge rather than choice
gold,
11 for wisdom is more precious than
rubies, and nothing you desire can
compare with her.
12 "I, wisdom, dwell together with
prudence; I possess knowledge

instead of ··· 대신에
I'll have tea instead of coffee, please. 커피 대신에 차를 마실 게요.

and discretion.
13 To fear the LORD is to hate evil;
I hate pride and arrogance, evil
behavior and perverse speech.
14 Counsel and sound judgment
are mine; I have insight, I have
power.
15 By me kings reign and rulers issue
decrees that are just;
16 by me princes govern, and nobles–
all who rule on earth.
17 I love those who love me, and those
who seek me find me.
18 With me are riches and honor,
enduring wealth and prosperity.
19 My fruit is better than fine gold; what

rule on …을 해결하다
Look, I can rule on this. 이것 봐 난 이거 해결할 수 있어.

I yield surpasses choice silver.
20 I walk in the way of righteousness,
along the paths of justice,
21 bestowing a rich inheritance on
those who love me and making
their treasuries full.
22 "The LORD brought me forth as the
first of his works, before his deeds
of old;
23 I was formed long ages ago, at the
very beginning, when the world
came to be.
24 When there were no watery depths,
I was given birth, when there were
no springs overflowing with water;
25 before the mountains were settled

bring forth …을 낳다[생산하다]
She brought forth a son. 그녀는 아들을 낳았다.

in place, before the hills, I was given
birth,
26 before he made the world or its
fields or any of the dust of the earth.
27 I was there when he set the heavens
in place, when he marked out the
horizon on the face of the deep,
28 when he established the clouds
above and fixed securely the
fountains of the deep,
29 when he gave the sea its boundary
so the waters would not overstep
his command, and when he
marked out the foundations of the
earth.
30 Then I was the constantly at his side.

mark out …을 표시하다[그리다]
Mark out the good and the bad. 선과 악을 가리다.

I was filled with delight day after
day, rejoicing always in his presence,
31 rejoicing in his whole world and
delighting in mankind.
32 "Now then, my children, listen to
me; blessed are those who keep
my ways.
33 Listen to my instruction and be
wise; do not disregard it.
34 Blessed are those who listen to me,
watching daily at my doors, waiting
at my doorway.
35 For those who find me find life and
receive favor from the LORD.
36 But those who fail to find me
harm themselves; all who hate me

wait at …에서 시중 들다
I will wait at the bus stop. 내가 버스 정류장에서 기다릴게요.

love death.

Proverbs 9장 1~18절

1 Wisdom has built her house; she has
set up its seven pillars.
2 She has prepared her meat and
mixed her wine; she has also set her
table.
3 She has sent out her servants, and
she calls from the highest point of
the city,
4 "Let all who are simple come to my
house!" To those who have no sense
she says,
5 "Come, eat my food and drink the

set up 건립하다, 준비하다
My aunt set up shop in downtown. 숙모가 시내에 개업했다.

wine I have mixed.
6 Leave your simple ways and you
will live; walk in the way of insight."
7 Whoever corrects a mocker invites
insults; whoever rebukes the wicked
incurs abuse.
8 Do not rebuke mockers or they will
hate you; rebuke the wise and they
will love you.
9 Instruct the wise and they will be
wiser still; teach the righteous and
they will add to their learning.
10 The fear of the LORD is the beginn-
ing of wisdom, and knowledge of
the Holy One is understanding.
11 For through wisdom your days will

walk in 안으로 들어가다
Let's walk in the grass. 잔디 위에서 걸어 보자.

be many, and years will be added
to your life.
12 If you are wise, your wisdom will
reward you; if you are a mocker, you
alone will suffer.
13 Folly is an unruly woman; she is
simple and knows nothing.
14 She sits at the door of her house, on
a seat at the highest point of the city,
15 calling out to those who pass by,
who go straight on their way,
16 "Let all who are simple come to my
house!" To those who have no sense
she says,
17 "Stolen water is sweet; food eaten
in secret is delicious!"

pass by 옆을 지나다, 지나치다
Does a school bus pass by here? 학교 버스가 이곳으로 지나가나요?

18 But little do they know that the
dead are there, that her guests are
deep in the realm of the dead.

Proverbs 10장 1~32절

1 The proverbs of Solomon: A wise
son brings joy to his father, but a
foolish son brings grief to his mother.
2 Ill-gotten treasures have no lasting
value, but righteousness delivers
from death.
3 The LORD does not let the righteous
go hungry, but he thwarts the
craving of the wicked.
4 Lazy hands make for poverty, but

deliver from …에서 구해내다
Deliver us from evil. 우리를 악에서 구하옵소서.

diligent hands bring wealth.
5 He who gathers crops in summer is a
prudent son, but he who sleeps
during harvest is a disgraceful son.
6 Blessings crown the head of the
righteous, but violence overwhelms
the mouth of the wicked.
7 The name of the righteous is used
in blessings, but the name of the
wicked will rot.
8 The wise in heart accept commands,
but a chattering fool comes to ruin.
9 Whoever walks in integrity walks
securely, but whoever takes crooked
paths will be found out.
10 Whoever winks maliciously causes

find out (조사하여) 발견하다, 생각해 내다
What if my parents find out? 우리 부모님이 아시면 어떡해?

grief, and a chattering fool comes
to ruin.
11 The mouth of the righteous is a
fountain of life, but the mouth of
the wicked conceals violence.
12 Hatred stirs up conflict, but love
covers over all wrongs.
13 Wisdom is found on the lips of
the discerning, but a rod is for the
back of one who has no sense.
14 The wise store up knowledge,
but the mouth of a fool invites ruin.
15 The wealth of the rich is their
fortified city, but poverty is the ruin
of the poor.
16 The wages of the righteous is life,

stir up 일으키다
It'll stir up a lot of noise. 그것은 많은 소음을 일으킬 것이다.

but the earnings of the wicked are
sin and death.
17 Whoever heeds discipline shows
the way to life, but whoever ignores
correction leads others astray.
18 Whoever conceals hatred with lying
lips and spreads slander is a fool.
19 Sin is not ended by multiplying
words, but the prudent hold their
tongues.
20 The tongue of the righteous is
choice silver, but the heart of the
wicked is of little value.
21 The lips of the righteous nourish
many, but fools die for lack of sense.
22 The blessing of the LORD brings

die for …을 위해 죽다
I would die for a cause. 대의명분을 위해 죽을 수 있어.

wealth, without painful toil for it.
23 A fool finds pleasure in wicked
schemes, but a person of under-
standing delights in wisdom.
24 What the wicked dread will overt-
ake them; what the righteous
desire will be granted.
25 When the storm has swept by, the
wicked are gone, but the righteous
stand firm forever.
26 As vinegar to the teeth and smoke
to the eyes, so are sluggards to
those who send them.
27 The fear of the LORD adds length to
life, but the years of the wicked are
cut short.

stand firm 꿋꿋하다, 꿈쩍 않는
We are going to stand firm. 우리는 단호한 입장을 취할 것이다.

28 The prospect of the righteous is
joy, but the hopes of the wicked
come to nothing.
29 The way of the LORD is a refuge for
the blameless, but it is the ruin of
those who do evil.
30 The righteous will never be upr-
ooted, but the wicked will not re-
main in the land.
31 From the mouth of the righteous
comes the fruit of wisdom, but a
perverse tongue will be silenced.
32 The lips of the righteous know
what finds favor, but the mouth of
the wicked only what is perverse.

find favor (with) 인기를 얻다
Tony found favor with his boss. 토니는 상사의 총애를 받았다.

Proverbs 11장 1~31절

1 The LORD detests dishonest scales,
but accurate weights find favor with
him.
2 When pride comes, then comes
disgrace, but with humility comes
wisdom.
3 The integrity of the upright guides
them, but the unfaithful are de-
stroyed by their duplicity.
4 Wealth is worthless in the day of
wrath, but righteousness delivers
from death.
5 The righteousness of the blameles-
s makes their paths straight, but the

with humility 겸손하게
He is doing his best with humility. 그는 겸손에 최선을 다하고 있다.

wicked are brought down by their
own wickedness.
6 The righteousness of the upright
delivers them, but the unfaithful
are trapped by evil desires.
7 Hopes placed in mortals die with
them; all the promise of their power
comes to nothing.
8 The righteous person is rescued
from trouble, and it falls on the
wicked instead.
9 With their mouths the godless destr-
oy their neighbors, but through
knowledge the righteous escape.
10 When the righteous prosper, the
city rejoices; when the wicked per-

rescue from …에서 구조하다
The house was rescued from demolition. 주택은 해체되지 않고 구제되었다.

ish, there are shouts of joy.
11 Through the blessing of the upright
a city is exalted, but by the mouth of
the wicked it is destroyed.
12 Whoever derides their neighbor
has no sense, but the one who has
understanding holds their tongue.
13 A gossip betrays a confidence, but
a trustworthy person keeps a secret.
14 For lack of guidance a nation falls,
but victory is won through many ad-
visers.
15 Whoever puts up security for a
stranger will surely suffer, but who-
ever refuses to shake hands in pledge
is safe.

keep a secret 비밀을 지키다
No one can keep a secret. 비밀을 지킬 수 있는 사람은 없다.

16 A kindhearted woman gains honor,
but ruthless men gain only wealth.
17 Those who are kind benefit thems-
elves, but the cruel bring ruin on
themselves.
18 A wicked person earns deceptive
wages, but the one who sows right-
eousness reaps a sure reward.
19 Truly the righteous attains life, but
whoever pursues evil finds death.
20 The LORD detests those whose
hearts are perverse, but he delights
in those whose ways are blameless.
21 Be sure of this: The wicked will not
go unpunished, but those who are
righteous will go free.

be sure of …에 확신을 가지다, …을 믿다
You may be sure of his honesty. 너는 그가 정직하다는 것을 믿어도 좋다.

22 Like a gold ring in a pig's snout is
a beautiful woman who shows no
discretion.
23 The desire of the righteous ends
only in good, but the hope of the
wicked only in wrath.
24 One person gives freely, yet gains
even more; another withholds
unduly, but comes to poverty.
25 A generous person will prosper;
whoever refreshes others will be
refreshed.
26 People curse the one who hoards
grain, but they pray God's blessing
on the one who is willing to sell.
27 Whoever seeks good finds favor, but

end in …로 끝나다
He came to an end in an accident. 그 사람은 사고로 사망했다.

evil comes to one who searches
for it.
28 Those who trust in their riches
will fall, but the righteous will thrive
like a green leaf.
29 Whoever brings ruin on their family
will inherit only wind, and the fool
will be servant to the wise.
30 The fruit of the righteous is a tree of
life, and the one who is wise saves
lives.
31 If the righteous receive their due on
earth, how much more the un-
godly and the sinner!

trust in …을 믿다
I have a lot of trust in him. 저는 그를 매우 신임하고 있어요.

Proverbs 12장 1~28절

1 Whoever loves discipline loves
knowledge, but whoever hates
correction is stupid.
2 Good people obtain favor from the
LORD, but he condemns those who
devise wicked schemes.
3 No one can be established through
wickedness, but the righteous can-
not be uprooted.
4 A wife of noble character is her
husband's crown, but a disgraceful
wife is like decay in his bones.
5 The plans of the righteous are just,
but the advice of the wicked is

cannot be …리가 없다
Its value cannot be measured by money. 그 가치는 돈으로 잴 수 없다.

deceitful.
6 The words of the wicked lie in wait
for blood, but the speech of the up-
right rescues them.
7 The wicked are overthrown and are
no more, but the house of the
righteous stands firm.
8 A person is praised according to
their prudence, and one with a
warped mind is despised.
9 Better to be a nobody and yet
have a servant than pretend to be
somebody and have no food.
10 The righteous care for the needs of
their animals, but the kindest acts of
the wicked are cruel.

pretend to …인 체하다
He does not pretend to scholarship. 그는 학식을 내세우지 않는다.

11 Those who work their land will have
abundant food, but those who
chase fantasies have no sense.
12 The wicked desire the stronghold of
evildoers, but the root of the
righteous endures.
13 Evildoers are trapped by their sinful
talk, and so the innocent escape
trouble.
14 From the fruit of their lips people
are filled with good things, and the
work of their hands brings them re-
ward.
15 The way of fools seems right to
them, but the wise listen to advice.
16 Fools show their annoyance at once,

be filled with …로 가득 차다
Books are filled with great stories. 책은 재미있는 이야기들로 가득하다.

but the prudent overlook an insult.
17 An honest witness tells the truth,
but a false witness tells lies.
18 The words of the reckless pierce
like swords, but the tongue of the
wise brings healing.
19 Truthful lips endure forever, but a
lying tongue lasts only a moment.
20 Deceit is in the hearts of those who
plot evil, but those who promote
peace have joy.
21 No harm overtakes the righteous,
but the wicked have their fill of trou-
ble.
22 The LORD detests lying lips, but
he delights in people who are

tell the truth 사실대로 말하다
She swore to tell the truth. 그녀는 진실을 말할 것을 맹세했다.

trustworthy.
23 The prudent keep their knowledge
to themselves, but a fool's heart
blurts out folly.
24 Diligent hands will rule, but laziness
ends in forced labor.
25 Anxiety weighs down the heart, but
a kind word cheers it up.
26 The righteous choose their friends
carefully, but the way of the wicked
leads them astray.
27 The lazy do not roast any game, but
the diligent feed on the riches of
the hunt.
28 In the way of righteousness there is
life; along that path is immortality.

weigh down …을 짓누르다
He is weighed down with guilt. 그는 죄책감에 짓눌리고 있다.

Proverbs 13장 1~25절

1 A wise son heeds his father's instr-
uction, but a mocker does not re-
spond to rebukes.
2 From the fruit of their lips people
enjoy good things, but the unfaith-
ful have an appetite for violence.
3 Those who guard their lips preserve
their lives, but those who speak
rashly will come to ruin.
4 A sluggard's appetite is never filled,
but the desires of the diligent are
fully satisfied.
5 The righteous hate what is false, but
the wicked make themselves a

respond to …에 대응하다
I didn't respond to his question. 나는 그의 질문에 응답하지 않았다.

stench and bring shame on them-
selves.
6 Righteousness guards the person of
integrity, but wickedness over-
throws the sinner.
7 One person pretends to be rich,
yet has nothing; another pretends
to be poor, yet has great wealth.
8 A person's riches may ransom their
life, but the poor cannot respond to
threatening rebukes.
9 The light of the righteous shines
brightly, but the lamp of the wicked
is snuffed out.
10 Where there is strife, there is pride,
but wisdom is found in those who

shine brightly 밝게 빛나다
Some types of jellyfish shine very brightly. 어떤 종류의 해파리는 매우 밝게 빛나요.

take advice.

11 Dishonest money dwindles away,
but whoever gathers money little
by little makes it grow.

12 Hope deferred makes the heart sick,
but a longing fulfilled is a tree of life.

13 Whoever scorns instruction will
pay for it, but whoever respects a
command is rewarded.

14 The teaching of the wise is a fount-
ain of life, turning a person from
the snares of death.

15 Good judgment wins favor, but the
way of the unfaithful leads to their
destruction.

16 All who are prudent act with

pay for 대금을 지불하다, 빚을 갚다
How much did you pay for your car? 차 얼마 주고 샀니?

knowledge, but fools expose their
folly.
17 A wicked messenger falls into
trouble, but a trustworthy envoy
brings healing.
18 Whoever disregards discipline
comes to poverty and shame, but
whoever heeds correction is hon-
ored.
19 A longing fulfilled is sweet to the
soul, but fools detest turning from
evil.
20 Walk with the wise and become
wise, for a companion of fools suf-
fers harm.
21 Trouble pursues the sinner, but the

fall into …에 빠지다, …에 서다
I let my hat fall into the water. 나는 모자를 강에 빠뜨렸다.

righteous are rewarded with good
things.
22 A good person leaves an inheritance
for their children's children, but a
sinner's wealth is stored up for the
righteous.
23 An unplowed field produces food
for the poor, but injustice sweeps it
away.
24 Whoever spares the rod hates
their children, but the one who
loves their children is careful to
discipline them.
25 The righteous eat to their hearts'
content, but the stomach of the
wicked goes hungry.

leave for …로 떠나다
The woman will leave for Japan on Wednesday. 여자는 수요일 일본으로 떠날 것이다.

Proverbs 14장 1~35절

1 The wise woman builds her house,
but with her own hands the foolish
one tears hers down.
2 Whoever fears the LORD walks
uprightly, but those who despise
him are devious in their ways.
3 A fool's mouth lashes out with pride,
but the lips of the wise protect
them.
4 Where there are no oxen, the
manger is empty, but from the
strength of an ox come abundant
harvests.
5 An honest witness does not deceive,

tear down …을 파괴하다, …을 비방하다
He will tear down old buildings. 그는 오래된 건물들을 허물 것이다.

but a false witness pours out lies.
6 The mocker seeks wisdom and finds
none, but knowledge comes easily
to the discerning.
7 Stay away from a fool, for you will
not find knowledge on their lips.
8 The wisdom of the prudent is to
give thought to their ways, but the
folly of fools is deception.
9 Fools mock at making amends for
sin, but goodwill is found among
the upright.
10 Each heart knows its own bitterness,
and no one else can share its joy.
11 The house of the wicked will be des-
troyed, but the tent of the upright

away from …에서 떠나서
I live far away from home. 나는 집에서 멀리 떨어져 산다.

will flourish.
12 There is a way that appears to be
right, but in the end it leads to death.
13 Even in laughter the heart may
ache, and rejoicing may end in grief.
14 The faithless will be fully repaid for
their ways, and the good rewarded
for theirs.
15 The simple believe anything, but
the prudent give thought to their
steps.
16 The wise fear the LORD and shun
evil, but a fool is hotheaded and yet
feels secure.
17 A quick-tempered person does fooli-
sh things, and the one who devises

give thought to …을 생각해 보다
Let's give some thought to their offer. 그들의 제의에 대해 생각을 좀 해 봅시다.

evil schemes is hated.
18 The simple inherit folly, but the
prudent are crowned with knowl-
edge.
19 Evildoers will bow down in the
presence of the good, and the
wicked at the gates of the righteous.
20 The poor are shunned even by their
neighbors, but the rich have many
friends.
21 It is a sin to despise one's neighbor,
but blessed is the one who is kind to
the needy.
22 Do not those who plot evil go astray?
But those who plan what is good
find love and faithfulness.

the needy 빈곤한 사람들
His heart moved him to help the needy. 동정심에 이끌려 어려운 사람들을 도왔다.

23 All hard work brings a profit, but
mere talk leads only to poverty.
24 The wealth of the wise is their
crown, but the folly of fools yields
folly.
25 A truthful witness saves lives, but a
false witness is deceitful.
26 Whoever fears the LORD has a
secure fortress, and for their chil-
dren it will be a refuge.
27 The fear of the LORD is a fountain
of life, turning a person from the
snares of death.
28 A large population is a king's glory,
but without subjects a prince is
ruined.

turn from [관찰 · 연구 따위]를 그만두다, 버리다
Nothing will turn him from his will. 누구도 그 놈 의지 못 꺾지.

29 Whoever is patient has great unders-
tanding, but one who is quick-tem-
pered displays folly.
30 A heart at peace gives life to the
body, but envy rots the bones.
31 Whoever oppresses the poor shows
contempt for their Maker, but who-
ever is kind to the needy honors
God.
32 When calamity comes, the wicked
are brought down, but even in death
the righteous seek refuge in God.
33 Wisdom reposes in the heart of
the discerning and even among
fools she lets herself be known.
34 Righteousness exalts a nation, but

in the heart of …의 한가운데에
Stay in the Heart of Times Square! 타임스퀘어의 중심에 머무르세요!

sin condemns any people.
35 A king delights in a wise servant,
but a shameful servant arouses his
fury.

Proverbs 15장 1~33절

1 A gentle answer turns away wrath,
but a harsh word stirs up anger.
2 The tongue of the wise adorns
knowledge, but the mouth of the
fool gushes folly.
3 The eyes of the LORD are everywhe-
re, keeping watch on the wicked
and the good.
4 The soothing tongue is a tree of life,

turn away 물리치다, 외면하다
I didn't turn away from you. 나는 너에게 등을 돌리지 않았다.

but a perverse tongue crushes the spirit.

5 A fool spurns a parent's discipline, but whoever heeds correction shows prudence.

6 The house of the righteous contains great treasure, but the income of the wicked brings ruin.

7 The lips of the wise spread knowledge, but the hearts of fools are not upright.

8 The LORD detests the sacrifice of the wicked, but the prayer of the upright pleases him.

9 The LORD detests the way of the wicked, but he loves those who

detest 몹시 싫어하다, 혐오하다
I detest that kind of scene. 나는 그런 종류의 장면을 싫어한다.

pursue righteousness.
10 Stern discipline awaits anyone who
leaves the path; the one who hates
correction will die.
11 Death and Destruction lie open
before the LORD—how much more
do human hearts!
12 Mockers resent correction, so they
avoid the wise.
13 A happy heart makes the face
cheerful, but heartache crushes the
spirit.
14 The discerning heart seeks knowle-
dge, but the mouth of a fool feeds
on folly.
15 All the days of the oppressed are

feed on …을 먹고 살다
They feed on nectar or leaves. 그들은 꿀이나 잎을 먹이로 먹습니다.

wretched, but the cheerful heart
has a continual feast.
16 Better a little with the fear of the
LORD than great wealth with
turmoil.
17 Better a small serving of vegetables
with love than a fattened calf with
hatred.
18 A hot-tempered person stirs up
conflict, but the one who is patient
calms a quarrel.
19 The way of the sluggard is blocked
with thorns, but the path of the
upright is a highway.
20 A wise son brings joy to his father,
but a foolish man despises his

hot-tempered 욱하는 성미가 있는
No one likes a hot-tempered person! 아무도 욱하는 사람을 좋아하지 않습니다!

mother.
21 Folly brings joy to one who has no
sense, but whoever has understand-
ing keeps a straight course.
22 Plans fail for lack of counsel, but
with many advisers they succeed.
23 A person finds joy in giving an apt
reply–and how good is a timely
word!
24 The path of life leads upward for
the prudent to keep them from
going down to the realm of the
dead.
25 The LORD tears down the house of
the proud, but he sets the widow's
boundary stones in place.

for lack of …이 부족해서
The tree died for lack of water. 그 나무는 물이 부족해서 죽었다.

26 The LORD detests the thoughts of
the wicked, but gracious words are
pure in his sight.
27 The greedy bring ruin to their
households, but the one who hates
bribes will live.
28 The heart of the righteous weighs
its answers, but the mouth of the
wicked gushes evil.
29 The LORD is far from the wicked, but
he hears the prayer of the righteous.
30 Light in a messenger's eyes brings
joy to the heart, and good news
gives health to the bones.
31 Whoever heeds life-giving correct-
ion will be at home among the wise.

life-giving 생명[생기]을 주는, 살아 있게 하는
It is both powerful and life giving. 그 길은 강력하며 생명을 주는 것이기도 하다.

32 Those who disregard discipline
despise themselves, but the one
who heeds correction gains under-
standing.
33 Wisdom's instruction is to fear the
LORD, and humility comes before
honor.

come before …앞에 나타나다[출석하다]
Spring has come before I knew it. 어느새 봄이 왔다.

NIV개정

지혜의 성경 영어 잠언 따라쓰기 1

부록

잠언 1장~15장 / 원어민 발음 / 한글개역개정 수록

✦ 알파벳 대문자, 소문자, 발음기호와 발음

A a [eɪ] 에이	**B b** [biː] 비	**C c** [siː] 시	**D d** [diː] 디
E e [iː] 이	**F f** [ef] 에프	**G g** [dʒiː] 지	**H h** [eɪtʃ] 에이치
I i [aɪ] 아이	**J j** [dʒeɪ] 제이	**K k** [keɪ] 케이	**L l** [el] 엘
M m [em] 엠	**N n** [en] 엔	**O o** [oʊ] 오	**P p** [piː] 피
Q q [kjuː] 큐	**R r** [ɑː(r)] 아르	**S s** [es] 에스	**T t** [tiː] 티
U u [juː] 유	**V v** [viː] 브이	**W w** [ˈdʌbljuː] 더블유	**X x** [eks] 엑스
Y y [waɪ] 와이	**Z z** [zed/ziː] 지		

Proverbs 잠언

1장 1 The proverbs of Solomon son of David, king of Israel:
더 프라버브즈 어브 살러먼 선 어브 데이비드, 킹 어브 이즈리얼
다윗의 아들 이스라엘 왕 솔로몬의 잠언이라

2 for gaining wisdom and instruction; for understanding words of insight;
포어 게이닝 위즈덤 언드 인스트럭션 포어 언더스탠딩 워즈 어브 인사이트
이는 지혜와 훈계를 알게 하며 명철의 말씀을 깨닫게 하며

3 for receiving instruction in prudent behavior, doing what is right and just and fair;
포어 러시빙 인스트럭션 인 프루던트 비헤이브여, 두잉 윗 이즈 라이트 언드 저스트 언드 페어
지혜롭게, 공의롭게, 정의롭게, 정직하게 행할 일에 대하여 훈계를 받게 하며

4 for giving prudence to those who are simple, knowledge and discretion to the young—
포어 기빙 프루던스 투 도우즈 후 아아 심펄, 날러지 언드 디스크레션 투 더 영
어리석은 자를 슬기롭게 하며 젊은 자에게 지식과 근신함을 주기 위한 것이니

5 let the wise listen and add to their learning, and let the discerning get guidance—
렛 더 와이즈 리선 언드 애드 투 데어 러닝, 언드 렛 더 디서닝 겟 가이던스
지혜 있는 자는 듣고 학식이 더할 것이요 명철한 자는 지략을 얻을 것이라

6 for understanding proverbs and parables, the sayings and riddles of the wise.
포어 언더스탠딩 프라버브즈 언드 페어러벌즈, 더 세이잉즈 언드 리덜즈 어브 더 와이즈.
잠언과 비유와 지혜 있는 자의 말과 그 오묘한 말을 깨달으리라

7 The fear of the LORD is the beginning of knowledge, but fools despise wisdom and instruction.
더 피어 어브 더 로어드 이즈 더 비기닝 어브 날러지, 벗 풀즈 디스파이즈 위즈덤 언드 인스트럭션.
여호와를 경외하는 것이 지식의 근본이거늘 미련한 자는 지혜와 훈계를 멸시하느니라

8 Listen, my son, to your father's instruction and do not forsake your mother's teaching.
리선, 마이 선, 투 요어 파더즈 인스트럭션 언드 두 낫 포어세익 요어 머더즈 티칭.
내 아들아 네 아비의 훈계를 들으며 네 어미의 법을 떠나지 말라

9 They are a garland to grace your head and a chain to adorn your neck.
데이 아아 어 가얼런드 투 그레이스 요어 헤드 언드 어 체인 투 어돈 요어 넥.
이는 네 머리의 아름다운 관이요 네 목의 금 사슬이니라

10 My son, if sinful men entice you, do not give in to them.
마이 선, 이프 신펄 멘 인타이스 유, 두 낫 기브 인 투 뎀.
내 아들아 악한 자가 너를 꾈지라도 따르지 말라

11 If they say, "Come along with us; let's lie in wait for innocent blood, let's ambush some harmless soul;
이프 데이 세이, 컴 얼롱 윋 어스 렛스 라이 인 웨잇 포어 이너선트 블러드, 렛스 앰부쉬 섬 함러스 소울
그들이 네게 말하기를 우리와 함께 가자 우리가 가만히 엎드렸다가 사람의 피를 흘리자 죄 없는 자를 까닭 없이
숨어 기다리다가

12 let's swallow them alive, like the grave, and whole, like those who go down to the pit;
렛스 스왈로우 뎀 얼라이브, 라익 더 그레이브, 언드 호울, 라익 도우즈 후 고우 다운 투 더 핏
스올 같이 그들을 산 채로 삼키며 무덤에 내려가는 자들 같이 통으로 삼키자

13 we will get all sorts of valuable things and fill our houses with plunder;
위 윌 겟 올 소어트스 어브 밸려벌 씽즈 언드 필 아우어 하우서즈 윋 플런더
우리가 온갖 보화를 얻으며 빼앗은 것으로 우리 집을 채우리니

14 cast lots with us; we will all share the loot"—
캐스트 랏스 윋 어스, 위 윌 올 셰어 더 룻
너는 우리와 함께 제비를 뽑고 우리가 함께 전대 하나만 두자 할지라도

15 my son, do not go along with them, do not set foot on their paths;
마이 선, 두 낫 고우 얼롱 윋 뎀, 두 낫 셋 풋 안 데어 팬즈
내 아들아 그들과 함께 길에 다니지 말라 네 발을 금하여 그 길을 밟지 말라

16 for their feet rush into evil, they are swift to shed blood.
포어 데어 핏 러쉬 인투 이벌, 데이 아아 스위프트 투 셰드 블러드.
대저 그 발은 악으로 달려가며 피를 흘리는 데 빠름이니라

17 How useless to spread a net where every bird can see it!
하우 유슬러스 투 스프레드 어 넷 웨어 에브리 버드 캔 시 잇!
새가 보는 데서 그물을 치면 헛일이겠거늘

18 These men lie in wait for their own blood; they ambush only themselves!
디즈 멘 라이 인 웨잇 포어 데어 오운 블러드 데이 앰부쉬 오운리 뎀셀브즈!
그들이 가만히 엎드림은 자기의 피를 흘릴 뿐이요 숨어 기다림은 자기의 생명을 해할 뿐이니

19 Such are the paths of all who go after ill-gotten gain; it takes away the life of those who get it.
서치 아아 더 팬즈 어브 올 후 고우 애프터 일가턴 게인 잇 테익스 어웨이 더 라이프 어브 도우즈 후 겟 잇.
이익을 탐하는 모든 자의 길은 다 이러하여 자기의 생명을 잃게 하느니라

20 Out in the open wisdom calls aloud, she raises her voice in the public square;
아웃 인 디 오우펀 위즈덤 콜즈 얼라우드, 쉬 레이저즈 허 보이스 인 더 퍼블릭 스퀘
지혜가 길거리에서 부르며 광장에서 소리를 높이며

21 on top of the wall she cries out, at the city gate she makes her speech:
안 탑 어브 더 월 쉬 크라이즈 아웃, 앳 더 시티 게이트 쉬 메익스 허 스피치
시끄러운 길목에서 소리를 지르며 성문 어귀와 성중에서 그 소리를 발하여 이르되

22 "How long will you who are simple love your simple ways? How long will mockers delight in mockery and fools hate knowledge?
하우 롱 윌 유 후 아아 심펄 러브 요어 심펄 웨이즈? 하우 롱 윌 마커즈 딜랏 인 마커리 언드 풀즈 헤이트 날러지?
너희 어리석은 자들은 어리석음을 좋아하며 거만한 자들은 거만을 기뻐하며 미련한 자들은 지식을 미워하니 어느 때까지 하겠느냐

23 Repent at my rebuke! Then I will pour out my thoughts to you, I will make known to you my teachings.
리펜트 앳 마이 리뷰! 덴 아이 윌 포어 아웃 마이 쏫스 투 유, 아이 윌 메익 노운 투 유 마이 티칭즈.
나의 책망을 듣고 돌이키라 보라 내가 나의 영을 너희에게 부어 주며 내 말을 너희에게 보이리라

24 But since you refuse to listen when I call and no one pays attention when I stretch out my hand,
벗 신스 유 레퓨즈 투 리선 웬 아이 콜 언드 노우 원 페이즈 어텐션 웬 아이 스트레치 아웃 마이 핸드.
내가 불렀으나 너희가 듣기 싫어하였고 내가 손을 폈으나 돌아보는 자가 없었고

25 since you disregard all my advice and do not accept my rebuke,
신스 유 디스리가아드 올 마이 애드바이스 언드 두 낫 억셉트 마이 리뷰.
도리어 나의 모든 교훈을 멸시하며 나의 책망을 받지 아니하였은즉

26 I in turn will laugh when disaster strikes you; I will mock when calamity overtakes you—
아이 인 턴 윌 래프 웬 디재스터 스트라익스 유 아이 윌 막 웬 컬래머티 오우버테익스 유
너희가 재앙을 만날 때에 내가 웃을 것이며 너희에게 두려움이 임할 때에 내가 비웃으리라

27 when calamity overtakes you like a storm, when disaster sweeps over you like a whirlwind, when distress and trouble overwhelm you.
웬 컬래머티 오우버테익스 유 라익 어 스톰, 웬 디재스터 스윕스 오우버 유 라익 어 월륀드, 웬 디스트레스 언드 트러벌 오우버웰므 유.
너희의 두려움이 광풍 같이 임하겠고 너희의 재앙이 폭풍 같이 이르겠고 너희에게 근심과 슬픔이 임하리니

28 "Then they will call to me but I will not answer; they will look for me but will not find me,
덴 데이 윌 콜 투 미 벗 아이 윌 낫 앤서 데이 윌 룩 포어 미 벗 윌 낫 파인드 미,
그 때에 너희가 나를 부르리라 그래도 내가 대답하지 아니하겠고 부지런히 나를 찾으리라 그래도 나를 만나지 못하리니

29 since they hated knowledge and did not choose to fear the LORD.
신스 데이 헤이터드 날러지 언드 디드 낫 추즈 투 피어 더 로어드.
대저 너희가 지식을 미워하며 여호와 경외하기를 즐거워하지 아니하며

30 Since they would not accept my advice and spurned my rebuke,
신스 데이 워드 낫 억셉트 마이 애드바이스 언드 스펀드 마이 리뷰,
나의 교훈을 받지 아니하고 나의 모든 책망을 업신여겼음이니라

31 they will eat the fruit of their ways and be filled with the fruit of their schemes.
데이 윌 잇 더 프룻 어브 데어 웨이즈 언드 비 필드 윋 더 프룻 어브 데어 스킴즈.
그러므로 자기 행위의 열매를 먹으며 자기 꾀에 배부르리라

32 For the waywardness of the simple will kill them, and the complacency of fools will destroy them;
포어 더 웨이워드너스 어브 더 심펄 윌 킬 뎀, 언드 더 컴플레이선시 어브 풀즈 윌 디스트로이 뎀
어리석은 자의 퇴보는 자기를 죽이며 미련한 자의 안일은 자기를 멸망시키려니와

33 but whoever listens to me will live in safety and be at ease, without fear of harm."
벗 후에버 리선즈 투 미 윌 리브 인 세이프티 언드 비 앳 이즈, 위다우트 피어 어브 함.
오직 내 말을 듣는 자는 평안히 살며 재앙의 두려움이 없이 안전하리라

proverb [právəːrb] n. 잠언
gain [gein] vt. 얻다, 획득하다
insight [insàit] n. 통찰, 간파
prudent [prúːdənt] a. 분별 있는
behavior [bihéivjər] n. 행동, 행실
parable [pǽrəbəl] n. 우화, 비유
riddle [rídl] n. 수수께끼
despise [dispáiz] vt. 경멸하다
forsake [fərséik] vt. 버리다
garland [gáːrlənd] n. 화환, 화관
adorn [ədɔ́ːrn] vt. 장식하다
entice [entáis] vt. 유혹하다
innocent [ínəsnt] a. 순결한
ambush [ǽmbuʃ] n. 잠복, 매복
swallow [swálou] vt. 삼키다
plunder [plʌ́ndər] vt. 약탈하다
pit [pit] n. 구덩이, 구멍
sweep [swiːp] vt. 청소하다
loot [luːt] n. 약탈물, 전리품
square [skwɛər] n. 광장
simple [símpəl] a. 어리석은
mockery [mákəri] n. 비웃음
disaster [dizǽstər] n. 천재, 재난
scheme [skiːm] n. 계획, 기획

2장 1 My son, if you accept my words and store up my commands within you,
마이 선, 이프 유 억셉트 마이 워즈 언드 스토어 업 마이 커맨즈 위씬 유.
내 아들아 네가 만일 나의 말을 받으며 나의 계명을 네게 간직하며

2 turning your ear to wisdom and applying your heart to understanding—
터닝 요어 이어 투 위즈덤 언드 업라이잉 요어 하아트 투 언더스탠딩
네 귀를 지혜에 기울이며 네 마음을 명철에 두며

3 indeed, if you call out for insight and cry aloud for understanding,
인디드, 이프 유 콜 아웃 포어 인사이트 언드 크라이 얼라우드 포어 언더스탠딩.
지식을 불러 구하며 명철을 얻으려고 소리를 높이며

4 and if you look for it as for silver and search for it as for hidden treasure,
언드 이프 유 룩 포어 잇 애즈 포어 실버 언드 서치 포어 잇 애즈 포어 히던 트레저.
은을 구하는 것 같이 그것을 구하며 감추어진 보배를 찾는 것 같이 그것을 찾으면

5 then you will understand the fear of the LORD and find the knowledge of God.
덴 유 윌 언더스탠드 더 피어 어브 더 로어드 언드 파인드 더 날러지 어브 가드.
여호와 경외하기를 깨달으며 하나님을 알게 되리니

6 For the LORD gives wisdom; from his mouth come knowledge and understanding.
포어 더 로어드 기브즈 위즈덤 프럼 히즈 마우쓰 컴 날러지 언드 언더스탠딩.
대저 여호와는 지혜를 주시며 지식과 명철을 그 입에서 내심이며

7 He holds success in store for the upright, he is a shield to those whose walk is blameless,
히 호울즈 석세스 인 스토어 포어 디 업라이트, 히 이즈 어 쉴드 투 도우즈 후즈 웍 이즈 블레임러스,
그는 정직한 자를 위하여 완전한 지혜를 예비하시며 행실이 온전한 자에게 방패가 되시나니

8 for he guards the course of the just and protects the way of his faithful ones.
포어 히 가아즈 더 코어스 어브 더 저스트 언드 프러텍트스 더 웨이 어브 히즈 페이쓰펄 원즈.
대저 그는 정의의 길을 보호하시며 그의 성도들의 길을 보전하려 하심이니라

9 Then you will understand what is right and just and fair—every good path.
덴 유 윌 언더스탠드 윗 이즈 라이트 언드 저스트 언드 페어 에브리 구드 패쓰.
그런즉 네가 공의와 정의와 정직 곧 모든 선한 길을 깨달을 것이라

10 For wisdom will enter your heart, and knowledge will be pleasant to your soul.
포어 위즈덤 윌 엔터 요어 하아트, 언드 날러지 윌 비 플레전트 투 요어 소울.
곧 지혜가 네 마음에 들어가며 지식이 네 영혼을 즐겁게 할 것이요

11 Discretion will protect you, and understanding will guard you.
디스크레션 윌 프러텍트 유, 언드 언더스탠딩 윌 가아드 유.
근신이 너를 지키며 명철이 너를 보호하여

12 Wisdom will save you from the ways of wicked men, from men whose words are perverse,
위즈덤 윌 세이브 유 프럼 더 웨이즈 어브 위커드 멘, 프럼 멘 후즈 워즈 아아 퍼버스,
악한 자의 길과 패역을 말하는 자에게서 건져 내리라

13 who have left the straight paths to walk in dark ways,
후 해브 레프트 더 스트레이트 팻즈 투 웍 인 다아크 웨이즈,

이 무리는 정직한 길을 떠나 어두운 길로 행하며

14 who delight in doing wrong and rejoice in the perverseness of evil,
후 딜랏 인 두잉 롱 언드 리조이스 인 더 퍼버스너스 어브 이벌,
행악하기를 기뻐하며 악인의 패역을 즐거워하나니

15 whose paths are crooked and who are devious in their ways.
후즈 팬즈 아아 크루커드 언드 후 아아 디비어스 인 데어 웨이즈.
그 길은 구부러지고 그 행위는 패역하니라

16 Wisdom will save you also from the adulterous woman, from the wayward woman with her seductive words,
위즈덤 윌 세이브 유 올소우 프럼 디 어덜터러스 워먼, 프럼 더 웨이워드 워먼 윋 허 시덕티브 워즈,
지혜가 또 너를 음녀에게서, 말로 호리는 이방 계집에게서 구원하리니

17 who has left the partner of her youth and ignored the covenant she made before God.
후 해즈 레프트 더 파아트너 어브 허 유쓰 언드 이그노어드 더 커버넌트 쉬 메이드 비포어 가드.
그는 젊은 시절의 짝을 버리며 그의 하나님의 언약을 잊어버린 자라

18 Surely her house leads down to death and her paths to the spirits of the dead.
슈얼리 허 하우스 리즈 다운 투 데쓰 언드 허 팬즈 투 더 스피릿스 어브 더 데드.
그의 집은 사망으로, 그의 길은 스올로 기울어졌나니

19 None who go to her return or attain the paths of life.
넌 후 고우 투 허 리턴 오어 어테인 더 팬즈 어브 라이프.
누구든지 그에게로 가는 자는 돌아오지 못하며 또 생명 길을 얻지 못하느니라

20 Thus you will walk in the ways of the good and keep to the paths of the righteous.
더스 유 윌 웍 인 더 웨이즈 어브 더 구드 언드 킵 투 더 팬즈 어브 더 라이처스.
지혜가 너를 선한 자의 길로 행하게 하며 또 의인의 길을 지키게 하리니

21 For the upright will live in the land, and the blameless will remain in it;
포어 디 업라이트 윌 라이브 인 더 랜드, 언드 더 블레임러스 윌 리메인 인 잇
대저 정직한 자는 땅에 거하며 완전한 자는 땅에 남아 있으리라

22 but the wicked will be cut off from the land, and the unfaithful will be torn from it.
벗 더 위커드 윌 비 컷 오프 프럼 더 랜드, 언드 디 언페이쓰펄 윌 비 톤 프럼 잇.
그러나 악인은 땅에서 끊어지겠고 간사한 자는 땅에서 뽑히리라

accept [æksépt] vt. 받아들이다
wisdom [wízdəm] n. 현명함, 지혜
apply [əplái] vt. 적용하다
indeed [indíːd] ad. 참으로
fear [fiər] n. 두려움, 무서움
upright [ʌ́pràit] a. 똑바로, 곧은
shield [ʃiːld] n. 방패, 보호물
soul [soul] n. (영)혼, 정신
guard [gɑːrd] n. 경계, 망보기
protect [prətékt] vt. 보호하다
wicked [wíkid] a. 악한, 사악한
straight [streit] a. 곧은, 일직선의
delight [diláit] n. 기쁨, 즐거움
rejoice [ridʒɔ́is] vi. 기뻐하다
crooked [krúkid] a. 꼬부라진
devious [díːviəs] a. 교활한
save [seiv] vt. 구하다
seductive [sidʌ́ktiv] a. 유혹하는
covenant [kʌ́vənənt] n. 계약, 서약
ignore [ignɔ́ːr] vt. 무시하다
attain [ətéin] vt. 도달하다
path [pæθ] n. 길, 작은 길
land [lænd] n. 뭍, 육지
remain [riméin] vi. 남다

3장 1 My son, do not forget my teaching, but keep my commands in your heart,
마이 선, 두 낫 퍼겟 마이 티칭, 벗 킵 마이 커맨즈 인 요어 하아트,
내 아들아 나의 법을 잊어버리지 말고 네 마음으로 나의 명령을 지키라

2 for they will prolong your life many years and bring you peace and prosperity.
포어 데이 윌 프럴롱 요어 라이프 메니 이어즈 언드 브링 유 피스 언드 프라스페러티.
그리하면 그것이 네가 장수하여 많은 해를 누리게 하며 평강을 더하게 하리라

3 Let love and faithfulness never leave you; bind them around your neck, write them on the tablet of your heart.
렛 러브 언드 페이쓰펄네스 네버 리브 유 바인드 뎀 어라운드 요어 넥, 라이트 뎀 안 더 태블럿 어브 요어 하아트.
인자와 진리가 네게서 떠나지 말게 하고 그것을 네 목에 매며 네 마음판에 새기라

4 Then you will win favor and a good name in the sight of God and man.
덴 유 윌 윈 페이버 언드 어 구드 네임 인 더 사이트 어브 가드 언드 맨.
그리하면 네가 하나님과 사람 앞에서 은총과 귀중히 여김을 받으리라

5 Trust in the LORD with all your heart and lean not on your own understanding;
트러스트 인 더 로어드 윋 올 요어 하아트 언드 린 낫 안 요어 오운 언더스탠딩
너는 마음을 다하여 여호와를 신뢰하고 네 명철을 의지하지 말라

6 in all your ways submit to him, and he will make your paths straight.
인 올 요어 웨이즈 서브밋 투 힘, 언드 히 윌 메익 요어 팯즈 스트레이트.
너는 범사에 그를 인정하라 그리하면 네 길을 지도하시리라

7 Do not be wise in your own eyes; fear the LORD and shun evil.
두 낫 비 와이즈 인 요어 오운 아이즈 피어 더 로어드 언드 션 이벌.
스스로 지혜롭게 여기지 말지어다 여호와를 경외하며 악을 떠날지어다

8 This will bring health to your body and nourishment to your bones.
디스 윌 브링 헬쓰 투 요어 바디 언드 너리쉬먼트 투 요어 보운즈.
이것이 네 몸에 양약이 되어 네 골수를 윤택하게 하리라

9 Honor the LORD with your wealth, with the firstfruits of all your crops;
아너 더 로어드 윋 요어 웰쓰, 윋 더 퍼스트프룻스 어브 올 요어 크랍스
네 재물과 네 소산물의 처음 익은 열매로 여호와를 공경하라

10 then your barns will be filled to overflowing, and your vats will brim over with new wine.
덴 요어 반즈 윌 비 필드 투 오우버플로우잉, 언드 요어 뱃스 윌 브림 오우버 윋 누 와인.
그리하면 네 창고가 가득히 차고 네 포도즙 틀에 새 포도즙이 넘치리라

11 My son, do not despise the LORD's discipline, and do not resent his rebuke,
마이 선, 두 낫 디스파이즈 더 로어즈 디서플런, 언드 두 낫 리젠트 히즈 리뷰.
내 아들아 여호와의 징계를 경히 여기지 말라 그 꾸지람을 싫어하지 말라

12 because the LORD disciplines those he loves, as a father the son he delights in.
비카즈 더 로어드 디서플런즈 도우즈 히 러브즈, 애즈 어 파더 더 선 히 딜랏스 인.
대저 여호와께서 그 사랑하시는 자를 징계하시기를 마치 아비가 그 기뻐하는 아들을 징계함 같이 하시느니라

13 Blessed are those who find wisdom, those who gain understanding,

블레스트 아아 도우즈 후 파인드 위즈덤, 도우즈 후 게인 언더스탠딩.
지혜를 얻은 자와 명철을 얻은 자는 복이 있나니

14 for she is more profitable than silver and yields better returns than gold.
포어 쉬 이즈 모어 프라퍼터벌 던 실버 언드 일즈 베터 리턴즈 던 고울드.
이는 지혜를 얻는 것이 은을 얻는 것보다 낫고 그 이익이 정금보다 나음이니라

15 She is more precious than rubies; nothing you desire can compare with her.
쉬 이즈 모어 프레셔스 던 루비즈 너씽 유 디자여 캔 컴페어 윋 허.
지혜는 진주보다 귀하니 네가 사모하는 모든 것으로도 이에 비교할 수 없도다

16 Long life is in her right hand; in her left hand are riches and honor.
롱 라이프 이즈 인 허 라이트 핸드 인 허 레프트 핸드 아아 리처즈 언드 아너.
그의 오른손에는 장수가 있고 그의 왼손에는 부귀가 있나니

17 Her ways are pleasant ways, and all her paths are peace.
허 웨이즈 아아 플레전트 웨이즈, 언드 올 허 팬즈 아아 피스.
그 길은 즐거운 길이요 그의 지름길은 다 평강이니라

18 She is a tree of life to those who take hold of her; those who hold her fast will be blessed.
쉬 이즈 어 트리 어브 라이프 투 도우즈 후 테익 호울드 어브 허 도우즈 후 호울드 허 패스트 윌 비 블레스트.
지혜는 그 얻은 자에게 생명 나무라 지혜를 가진 자는 복되도다

19 By wisdom the LORD laid the earth's foundations, by understanding he set the heavens in place;
바이 위즈덤 더 로어드 레이드 디 어쓰스 파운데이션즈, 바이 언더스탠딩 히 셋 더 헤번즈 인 플레이스
여호와께서는 지혜로 땅에 터를 놓으셨으며 명철로 하늘을 견고히 세우셨고

20 by his knowledge the watery depths were divided, and the clouds let drop the dew.
바이 히즈 날러지 더 워터리 뎁쓰스 워 디바이디드, 언드 더 클라우즈 렛 드랍 더 두.
그의 지식으로 깊은 바다를 갈라지게 하셨으며 공중에서 이슬이 내리게 하셨느니라

21 My son, do not let wisdom and understanding out of your sight, preserve sound judgment and discretion;
마이 선, 두 낫 렛 위즈덤 언드 언더스탠딩 아웃 어브 요어 사이트, 프러저브 사운드 저지먼트 언드 디스크레션
내 아들아 완전한 지혜와 근신을 지키고 이것들이 네 눈 앞에서 떠나지 말게 하라

22 they will be life for you, an ornament to grace your neck.
데이 윌 비 라이프 포어 유, 앤 오어너먼트 투 그레이스 요어 넥.
그리하면 그것이 네 영혼의 생명이 되며 네 목에 장식이 되리니

23 Then you will go on your way in safety, and your foot will not stumble.
덴 유 윌 고우 안 요어 웨이 인 세이프티, 언드 요어 풋 윌 낫 스텀벌.
네가 네 길을 평안히 행하겠고 네 발이 거치지 아니하겠으며

24 When you lie down, you will not be afraid; when you lie down, your sleep will be sweet.
웬 유 라이 다운, 유 윌 낫 비 어프레이드 웬 유 라이 다운, 요어 슬립 윌 비 스윗.
네가 누울 때에 두려워하지 아니하겠고 네가 누운즉 네 잠이 달리로다

25 Have no fear of sudden disaster or of the ruin that overtakes the wicked,
해브 노우 피어 어브 서던 디재스터 오어 어브 더 루언 댓 오우버테익스 더 위커드,
너는 갑작스러운 두려움도 악인에게 닥치는 멸망도 두려워하지 말라

26 for the LORD will be at your side and will keep your foot from being snared.
포어 더 로어드 윌 비 앳 요어 사이드 언드 윌 킵 요어 풋 프럼 비잉 스네어드.
대저 여호와는 네가 의지할 이시니라 네 발을 지켜 걸리지 않게 하시리라

27 Do not withhold good from those to whom it is due, when it is in your power to act.
두 낫 위쓰호울드 구드 프럼 도우즈 투 훔 잇 이즈 듀, 웬 잇 이즈 인 요어 파워 투 액트.
네 손이 선을 베풀 힘이 있거든 마땅히 받을 자에게 베풀기를 아끼지 말며

28 Do not say to your neighbor, "Come back tomorrow and I'll give it to you"—when you already have it with you.
두 낫 세이 투 요어 네이버, 컴 백 터마아로우 언드 아일 기브 잇 투 유 웬 유 올레디 해브 잇 윋 유.
네게 있거든 이웃에게 이르기를 갔다가 다시 오라 내일 주겠노라 하지 말며

29 Do not plot harm against your neighbor, who lives trustfully near you.
두 낫 플랏 함 어겐스트 요어 네이버, 후 리브즈 트러스트펄리 니어 유.
네 이웃이 네 곁에서 평안히 살거든 그를 해하려고 꾀하지 말며

30 Do not accuse anyone for no reason—when they have done you no harm.
두 낫 어큐즈 에니원 포어 노우 리전 웬 데이 해브 던 유 노우 함.
사람이 네게 악을 행하지 아니하였거든 까닭 없이 더불어 다투지 말며

31 Do not envy the violent or choose any of their ways.
두 낫 엔비 더 바이얼런트 오어 추즈 에니 어브 데어 웨이즈.
포학한 자를 부러워하지 말며 그의 어떤 행위도 따르지 말라

32 For the LORD detests the perverse but takes the upright into his confidence.
포어 더 로어드 디테스트스 더 퍼버스 벗 테익스 디 업라이트 인투 히즈 칸퍼덴스.
대저 패역한 자는 여호와께서 미워하시나 정직한 자에게는 그의 교통하심이 있으며

33 The LORD's curse is on the house of the wicked, but he blesses the home of the righteous.
더 로어즈 커스 이즈 안 더 하우스 어브 더 위커드, 벗 히 블레시즈 더 호움 어브 더 라이처스.
악인의 집에는 여호와의 저주가 있거니와 의인의 집에는 복이 있느니라

34 He mocks proud mockers but shows favor to the humble and oppressed.
히 막스 프라우드 마커즈 벗 쇼우즈 페이버 투 더 험벌 언드 업레스트.
진실로 그는 거만한 자를 비웃으시며 겸손한 자에게 은혜를 베푸시나니

35 The wise inherit honor, but fools get only shame.
더 와이즈 인헤럿 아너, 벗 풀즈 겟 오운리 셰임.
지혜로운 자는 영광을 기업으로 받거니와 미련한 자의 영달함은 수치가 되느니라

forget [fərgét] vt. 잊다	submit [səbmít] vt. 복종시키다	blessed [blésid] a. 은총 입은
command [kəmǽnd] n. 명령, 호령	nourish [nə́ːriʃ] vt. 살지게 하다	profitable [prɑ́fitəbəl] a. 유리한
prolong [proulɔ́ːŋ] vt. 연장하다	shun [ʃʌn] vt. 피하다, 비키다	yield [jiːld] vt. 생기게 하다
peace [piːs] n. 평화, 태평	honor [ɑ́nər] n. 명예, 영예	precious [préʃəs] a. 비싼
prosperity [prɑspérəti] n. 번영	bone [boun] n. 뼈	stumble [stʌ́mbəl] vi. 넘어지다
faithful [féiθfəl] a. 충실한	barn [bɑːrn] n. 헛간, 광	snare [snεər] n. 덫, 올가미
sight [sait] n. 시각, 시력	brim [brim] n. 가장자리	plot [plɑt] n. 음모, 책략
lean [liːn] vi. 기대다	discipline [dísəplin] n. 훈련, 훈육	confidence [kɑ́nfidəns] n. 신용

4장 1 Listen, my sons, to a father's instruction; pay attention and gain understanding.
리선, 마이 선즈, 투 어 파더즈 인스트럭션 페이 어텐션 언드 게인 언더스탠딩.
아들들아 아비의 훈계를 들으며 명철을 얻기에 주의하라

2 I give you sound learning, so do not forsake my teaching.
아이 기브 유 사운드 러닝, 소우 두 낫 포어세익 마이 티칭.
내가 선한 도리를 너희에게 전하노니 내 법을 떠나지 말라

3 For I too was a son to my father, still tender, and cherished by my mother.
포어 아이 투 와즈 어 선 투 마이 파더, 스틸 텐더, 언드 체어리쉬트 바이 마이 머더.
나도 내 아버지에게 아들이었으며 내 어머니 보기에 유약한 외아들이었노라

4 Then he taught me, and he said to me, "Take hold of my words with all your heart; keep my commands, and you will live.
덴 히 톳 미, 언드 히 세드 투 미, 테익 호울드 어브 마이 워즈 윋 올 요어 하아트 킵 마이 커맨즈, 언드 유 윌 리브.
아버지가 내게 가르쳐 이르기를 내 말을 네 마음에 두라 내 명령을 지키라 그리하면 살리라

5 Get wisdom, get understanding; do not forget my words or turn away from them.
겟 위즈덤, 겟 언더스탠딩 두 낫 퍼겟 마이 워즈 오어 턴 어웨이 프럼 뎀
지혜를 얻으며 명철을 얻으라 내 입의 말을 잊지 말며 어기지 말라

6 Do not forsake wisdom, and she will protect you; love her, and she will watch over you.
두 낫 포어세익 위즈덤, 언드 쉬 윌 프러텍트 유 러브 허, 언드 쉬 윌 와치 오우버 유.
지혜를 버리지 말라 그가 너를 보호하리라 그를 사랑하라 그가 너를 지키리라

7 The beginning of wisdom is this: Get wisdom. Though it cost all you have, get understanding.
더 비기닝 어브 위즈덤 이즈 디스 겟 위즈덤 도우 잇 카스트 올 유 해브, 겟 언더스탠딩.
지혜가 제일이니 지혜를 얻으라 네가 얻은 모든 것을 가지고 명철을 얻을지니라

8 Cherish her, and she will exalt you; embrace her, and she will honor you.
체어리쉬 허, 언드 쉬 윌 이그졸트 유 엠브레이스 허, 언드 쉬 윌 아너 유.
그를 높이라 그리하면 그가 너를 높이 들리라 만일 그를 품으면 그가 너를 영화롭게 하리라

9 She will give you a garland to grace your head and present you with a glorious crown."
쉬 윌 기브 유 어 가얼런드 투 그레이스 요어 헤드 언드 프리젠트 유 윋 어 글로어리어스 크라운.
그가 아름다운 관을 네 머리에 두겠고 영화로운 면류관을 네게 주리라 하셨느니라

10 Listen, my son, accept what I say, and the years of your life will be many.
리선, 마이 선, 억셉트 웟 아이 세이, 언드 더 이어즈 어브 요어 라이프 윌 비 메니.
내 아들아 들으라 내 말을 받으라 그리하면 네 생명의 해가 길리라

11 I instruct you in the way of wisdom and lead you along straight paths.
아이 인스트럭트 유 인 더 웨이 어브 위즈덤 언드 리드 유 얼롱 스트레이트 팬즈.
내가 지혜로운 길을 네게 가르쳤으며 정직한 길로 너를 인도하였은즉

12 When you walk, your steps will not be hampered; when you run, you will not stumble.
웬 유 웍, 요어 스텝스 윌 낫 비 햄퍼드 웬 유 런, 유 윌 낫 스텀벌.
다닐 때에 네 걸음이 곤고하지 아니하겠고 달려갈 때에 실족하지 아니하리라

13 Hold on to instruction, do not let it go; guard it well, for it is your life.

호울드 안 투 인스트럭션, 두 낫 렛 잇 고우 가아드 잇 웰, 포어 잇 이즈 요어 라이프.
훈계를 굳게 잡아 놓치지 말고 지키라 이것이 네 생명이니라

14 Do not set foot on the path of the wicked or walk in the way of evildoers.
두 낫 셋 풋 안 더 패쓰 어브 더 위커드 오어 웍 인 더 웨이 어브 이벌두어즈.
사악한 자의 길에 들어가지 말며 악인의 길로 다니지 말지어다

15 Avoid it, do not travel on it; turn from it and go on your way.
어보이드 잇, 두 낫 트래벌 안 잇 턴 프럼 잇 언드 고우 안 요어 웨이.
그의 길을 피하고 지나가지 말며 돌이켜 떠나갈지어다

16 For they cannot rest until they do evil; they are robbed of sleep till they make someone stumble.
포어 데이 캐낫 레스트 언틸 데이 두 이벌 데이 아아 라브드 어브 슬립 틸 데이 메익 서뭔 스텀벌.
그들은 악을 행하지 못하면 자지 못하며 사람을 넘어뜨리지 못하면 잠이 오지 아니하며

17 They eat the bread of wickedness and drink the wine of violence.
데이 잇 더 브레드 어브 위커드너스 언드 드링크 더 와인 어브 바이얼런스.
불의의 떡을 먹으며 강포의 술을 마심이니라

18 The path of the righteous is like the morning sun, shining ever brighter till the full light of day.
더 패쓰 어브 더 라이처스 이즈 라익 더 모어닝 선, 샤이닝 에버 브라이터 틸 더 풀 라이트 어브 데이.
의인의 길은 돋는 햇살 같아서 크게 빛나 한낮의 광명에 이르거니와

19 But the way of the wicked is like deep darkness; they do not know what makes them stumble.
벗 더 웨이 어브 더 위커드 이즈 라익 딥 다아크너스 데이 두 낫 노우 웟 메익스 뎀 스텀벌.
악인의 길은 어둠 같아서 그가 걸려 넘어져도 그것이 무엇인지 깨닫지 못하느니라

20 My son, pay attention to what I say; turn your ear to my words.
마이 선, 페이 어텐션 투 웟 아이 세이 턴 요어 이어 투 마이 워즈.
내 아들아 내 말에 주의하며 내가 말하는 것에 네 귀를 기울이라

21 Do not let them out of your sight, keep them within your heart;
두 낫 렛 뎀 아웃 어브 요어 사이트, 킵 뎀 위씬 요어 하아트
그것을 네 눈에서 떠나게 하지 말며 네 마음 속에 지키라

22 for they are life to those who find them and health to one's whole body.
포어 데이 아아 라이프 투 도우즈 후 파인드 뎀 언드 헬쓰 투 원즈 호울 바디.
그것은 얻는 자에게 생명이 되며 그의 온 육체의 건강이 됨이니라

23 Above all else, guard your heart, for everything you do flows from it.
어버브 올 엘스, 가아드 요어 하아트, 포어 에브리씽 유 두 플로우즈 프럼 잇.
모든 지킬 만한 것 중에 더욱 네 마음을 지키라 생명의 근원이 이에서 남이니라

24 Keep your mouth free of perversity; keep corrupt talk far from your lips.
킵 요어 마우쓰 프리 어브 퍼버서티 킵 커럽트 톡 파아 프럼 요어 립스.
구부러진 말을 네 입에서 버리며 비뚤어진 말을 네 입술에서 멀리 하라

25 Let your eyes look straight ahead; fix your gaze directly before you.
렛 요어 아이즈 룩 스트레이트 어헤드 픽스 요어 게이즈 더렉틀리 비포어 유.
네 눈은 바로 보며 네 눈꺼풀은 네 앞을 곧게 살펴

26 Give careful thought to the paths for your feet and be steadfast in all your ways.
기브 케어펄 솟 투 더 팯즈 포어 요어 핏 언드 비 스테드패스트 인 올 요어 웨이즈.
네 발이 행할 길을 평탄하게 하며 네 모든 길을 든든히 하라

27 Do not turn to the right or the left; keep your foot from evil.
두 낫 턴 투 더 라이트 오어 더 레프트 킵 요어 풋 프럼 이벌.
좌로나 우로나 치우치지 말고 네 발을 악에서 떠나게 하라

instruction [instrʌ́kʃən] n. 훈계	embrace [embréis] vt. 얼싸안다	sleep [sli:p] vi. 잠자다
attention [əténʃən] n. 주의력	present [prizént] vt. 증정하다	violence [váiələns] n. 격렬함
tender [téndər] a. 썩기 쉬운	glorious [glɔ́:riəs] a. 영광스러운	bright [brait] a. 빛나는
heart [hɑ:rt] n. 심장, 마음	hampered [hǽmpər] vt. 방해하다	flow [flou] vi. 흐르다
watch [wɑtʃ] vt. 지켜보다	avoid [əvɔ́id] vt. 피하다, 회피하다	corrupt [kərʌ́pt] a. 부정한
cost [kɔ:st] n. 가격, 비용	travel [trǽvəl] vi. 여행하다	steadfast [stédfæ̀st] a. 확고부동한
cherish [tʃériʃ] vt. 소중히 하다	way [wei] n. 길, 도로	right [rait] a. 옳은, 올바른
exalt [igzɔ́:lt] vt. 높이다	rest [rest] n. 휴식, 휴게	left [left] a. 왼쪽의

5장 1 My son, pay attention to my wisdom, turn your ear to my words of insight,
마이 선, 페이 어텐션 투 마이 위즈덤, 턴 요어 이어 투 마이 워즈 어브 인사이트.
내 아들아 내 지혜에 주의하며 내 명철에 네 귀를 기울여서

2 that you may maintain discretion and your lips may preserve knowledge.
댓 유 메이 메인테인 디스크레션 언드 요어 립스 메이 프러저브 날러지.
근신을 지키며 네 입술로 지식을 지키도록 하라

3 For the lips of the adulterous woman drip honey, and her speech is smoother than oil;
포어 더 립스 어브 디 어덜터러스 워먼 드립 허니, 언드 허 스피치 이즈 스무더 던 오일
대저 음녀의 입술은 꿀을 떨어뜨리며 그의 입은 기름보다 미끄러우나

4 but in the end she is bitter as gall, sharp as a double-edged sword.
벗 인 디 엔드 쉬 이즈 비터 애즈 골, 샤아프 애즈 어 더벌에지드 소어드.
나중은 쑥 같이 쓰고 두 날 가진 칼 같이 날카로우며

5 Her feet go down to death; her steps lead straight to the grave.
허 핏 고우 다운 투 데쓰 허 스텝스 리드 스트레이트 투 더 그레이브.
그의 발은 사지로 내려가며 그의 걸음은 스올로 나아가나니

6 She gives no thought to the way of life; her paths wander aimlessly, but she does not know it.
쉬 기브즈 노우 솟 투 더 웨이 어브 라이프 허 팯즈 완더 에임러슬리, 벗 쉬 더즈 낫 노우 잇.
그는 생명의 평탄한 길을 찾지 못하며 자기 길이 든든하지 못하여도 그것을 깨닫지 못하느니라

7 Now then, my sons, listen to me; do not turn aside from what I say.
나우 덴, 마이 선즈, 리선 투 미 두 낫 턴 어사이드 프럼 웟 아이 세이.
그런즉 아들들아 나에게 들으며 내 입의 말을 버리지 말고

8 Keep to a path far from her, do not go near the door of her house,
킵 투 어 패쓰 파아 프럼 허, 두 낫 고우 니어 더 도어 어브 허 하우스.
네 길을 그에게서 멀리 하라 그의 집 문에도 가까이 가지 말라

9 lest you lose your honor to others and your dignity to one who is cruel,
레스트 유 루즈 요어 아너 투 어더즈 언드 요어 디그너티 투 원 후 이즈 크루얼.
두렵건대 네 존영이 남에게 잃어버리게 되며 네 수한이 잔인한 자에게 빼앗기게 될까 하노라

10 lest strangers feast on your wealth and your toil enrich the house of another.
레스트 스트레인저즈 피스트 안 요어 웰쓰 언드 요어 토일 엔리치 더 하우스 어브 어너더.
두렵건대 타인이 네 재물로 충족하게 되며 네 수고한 것이 외인의 집에 있게 될까 하노라

11 At the end of your life you will groan, when your flesh and body are spent.
앳 디 엔드 어브 요어 라이프 유 윌 그로운, 웬 요어 플레쉬 언드 바디 아아 스펜트.
두렵건대 마지막에 이르러 네 몸, 네 육체가 쇠약할 때에 네가 한탄하여

12 You will say, "How I hated discipline! How my heart spurned correction!
유 윌 세이, 하우 아이 헤이터드 디서플린! 하우 마이 하아트 스펀드 커렉션!
말하기를 내가 어찌하여 훈계를 싫어하며 내 마음이 꾸지람을 가벼이 여기고

13 I would not obey my teachers or turn my ear to my instructors.
아이 워드 낫 오우베이 마이 티처즈 오어 턴 마이 이어 투 마이 인스트럭터스.
내 선생의 목소리를 청종하지 아니하며 나를 가르치는 이에게 귀를 기울이지 아니하였던고

14 And I was soon in serious trouble in the assembly of God’s people."
언드 아이 와즈 순 인 시어리어스 트러벌 인 디 어셈블리 어브 가즈 피펄.
많은 무리들이 모인 중에서 큰 악에 빠지게 되었노라 하게 될까 염려하노라

15 Drink water from your own cistern, running water from your own well.
드링크 워터 프럼 요어 오운 시스턴, 러닝 워터 프럼 요어 오운 웰.
너는 네 우물에서 물을 마시며 네 샘에서 흐르는 물을 마시라

16 Should your springs overflow in the streets, your streams of water in the public squares?
슈드 요어 스프링즈 오우버플로우 인 더 스트릿스, 요어 스트림즈 어브 워터 인 더 퍼블릭 스퀘즈?
어찌하여 네 샘물을 집 밖으로 넘치게 하며 네 도랑물을 거리로 흘러가게 하겠느냐

17 Let them be yours alone, never to be shared with strangers.
렛 뎀 비 유어즈 얼로운, 네버 투 비 셰어드 윋 스트레인저즈.
그 물이 네게만 있게 하고 타인과 더불어 그것을 나누지 말라

18 May your fountain be blessed, and may you rejoice in the wife of your youth.
메이 요어 파운턴 비 블레스트, 언드 메이 유 리조이스 인 더 와이프 어브 요어 유쓰.
네 샘으로 복되게 하라 네가 젊어서 취한 아내를 즐거워하라

19 A loving doe, a graceful deer—may her breasts satisfy you always, may you ever be intoxicated with her love.
어 러빙 도우, 어 그레이스펄 디어 메이 허 브레스트스 새터스파이 유 올웨이즈, 메이 유 에버 비 인탁서케이터드 윋 허 러브.
그는 사랑스러운 암사슴 같고 아름다운 암노루 같으니 너는 그의 품을 항상 족하게 여기며 그의 사랑을 항상 연모하라

20 Why, my son, be intoxicated with another man's wife? Why embrace the bosom of a wayward woman?
와이, 마이 선, 비 인탁서케이터드 윋 어너더 맨즈 와이프? 와이 엠브레이스 더 부점 어브 어 웨이워드 워먼?

내 아들아 어찌하여 음녀를 연모하겠으며 어찌하여 이방 계집의 가슴을 안겠느냐

21 For your ways are in full view of the LORD, and he examines all your paths.
포어 요어 웨이즈 아아 인 풀 뷰 어브 더 로어드, 언드 히 이그재먼즈 올 요어 팬즈.
대저 사람의 길은 여호와의 눈 앞에 있나니 그가 그 사람의 모든 길을 평탄하게 하시느니라

22 The evil deeds of the wicked ensnare them; the cords of their sins hold them fast.
디 이벌 디즈 어브 더 위커드 인스네어 뎀 더 코어즈 어브 데어 신즈 호울드 뎀 패스트.
악인은 자기의 악에 걸리며 그 죄의 줄에 매이나니

23 For lack of discipline they will die, led astray by their own great folly.
포어 랙 어브 디서플런 데이 윌 다이, 레드 어스트레이 바이 데어 오운 그레이트 팔리.
그는 훈계를 받지 아니함으로 말미암아 죽겠고 심히 미련함으로 말미암아 혼미하게 되느니라

maintain [meintéin] vt. 지속하다
discretion [diskréʃən] n. 신중
preserve [prizə́ːrv] vt. 보전하다
knowledge [nάlidʒ] n. 지식
adulterous [ədʌ́ltərəs] a. 불의의
bitter [bítər] a. 쓴, 모진
gall [gɔːl] n. 담즙, 쓸개즙
sharp [ʃɑːrp] a. 날카로운
grave [greiv] n. 무덤, 분묘
sword [sɔːrd] n. 칼, 무력
dignity [dígnəti] n. 존엄, 위엄
cruel [krúːəl] a. 잔혹한
wealth [welθ] n. 부, 재산
toil [tɔil] n. 힘드는 일, 수고
enrich [enrítʃ] vt. 부유하게 만들다
groan [groun] vi. 신음하다
hate [heit] vt. 미워하다
obey [oubéi] vt. …에 복종하다
correction [kərékʃən] n. 정정
serious [síəriəs] a. 진지한
assembly [əsémbli] n. 집회
bosom [búzəm] n. 가슴
examine [igzǽmin] vt. 시험하다
astray [əstréi] ad. 타락하여

6장 1 My son, if you have put up security for your neighbor, if you have shaken hands in pledge for a stranger,
마이 선, 이프 유 해브 풋 업 시큐러티 포어 요어 네이버, 이프 유 해브 셰이컨 핸즈 인 플레지 포어 어 스트레인저.
내 아들아 네가 만일 이웃을 위하여 담보하며 타인을 위하여 보증하였으면

2 you have been trapped by what you said, ensnared by the words of your mouth.
유 해브 빈 트랩트 바이 윗 유 세드, 인스네어드 바이 더 워즈 어브 요어 마우쓰.
네 입의 말로 네가 얽혔으며 네 입의 말로 인하여 잡히게 되었느니라

3 So do this, my son, to free yourself, since you have fallen into your neighbor's hands: Go—to the point of exhaustion—and give your neighbor no rest!
소우 두 디스, 마이 선, 투 프리 요어셀프, 신스 유 해브 팔런 인투 요어 네이버즈 핸즈 고우 투 더 포인트 어브 이그조스천 언드 기브 요어 네이버 노우 레스트!
내 아들아 네가 네 이웃의 손에 빠졌은즉 이같이 하라 너는 곧 가서 겸손히 네 이웃에게 간구하여 스스로 구원하되

4 Allow no sleep to your eyes, no slumber to your eyelids.
얼라우 노우 슬립 투 요어 아이즈, 노우 슬럼버 투 요어 아일리즈.
네 눈을 잠들게 하지 말며 눈꺼풀을 감기게 하지 말고

5 Free yourself, like a gazelle from the hand of the hunter, like a bird from the snare of the fowler.
프리 요어셀프, 라익 어 거젤 프럼 더 핸드 어브 더 헌터, 라익 어 버드 프럼 더 스네어 어브 더 파울러.
노루가 사냥꾼의 손에서 벗어나는 것 같이, 새가 그물 치는 자의 손에서 벗어나는 것 같이 스스로 구원하라

6 Go to the ant, you sluggard; consider its ways and be wise!
고우 투 디 앤트, 유 슬러거드 컨시더 잇스 웨이즈 언드 비 와이즈!

게으른 자여 개미에게 가서 그가 하는 것을 보고 지혜를 얻으라

7 It has no commander, no overseer or ruler,

잇 해즈 노우 커맨더, 노우 오우버시어 오어 룰러.

개미는 두령도 없고 감독자도 없고 통치자도 없으되

8 yet it stores its provisions in summer and gathers its food at harvest.

옛 잇 스토어즈 잇스 프러비전즈 인 서머 언드 개더즈 잇스 푸드 앳 하아버스트.

먹을 것을 여름 동안에 예비하며 추수 때에 양식을 모으느니라

9 How long will you lie there, you sluggard? When will you get up from your sleep?

하우 롱 윌 유 라이 데어, 유 슬러거드? 웬 윌 유 겟 업 프럼 요어 슬립?

게으른 자여 네가 어느 때까지 누워 있겠느냐 네가 어느 때에 잠이 깨어 일어나겠느냐

10 A little sleep, a little slumber, a little folding of the hands to rest—

어 리털 슬립, 어 리털 슬럼버, 어 리털 포울딩 어브 더 핸즈 투 레스트

좀더 자자, 좀더 졸자, 손을 모으고 좀더 누워 있자 하면

11 and poverty will come on you like a thief and scarcity like an armed man.

언드 파버티 윌 컴 안 유 라익 어 씨프 언드 스케어시티 라익 앤 아아므드 맨.

네 빈궁이 강도 같이 오며 네 곤핍이 군사 같이 이르리라

12 A troublemaker and a villain, who goes about with a corrupt mouth,

어 트러벌메이커 언드 어 빌런, 후 고우즈 어바우트 윋 어 커럽트 마우쓰.

불량하고 악한 자는 구부러진 말을 하고 다니며

13 who winks maliciously with his eye, signals with his feet and motions with his fingers,

후 윙크스 멀리쉬슬리 윋 히즈 아이, 시그널즈 윋 히즈 핏 언드 모우션즈 윋 히즈 핑거즈,

눈짓을 하며 발로 뜻을 보이며 손가락질을 하며

14 who plots evil with deceit in his heart—he always stirs up conflict.

후 플랏스 이벌 윋 디싯 인 히즈 하아트 히 올웨이즈 스터즈 업 칸플릭트.

그의 마음에 패역을 품으며 항상 악을 꾀하여 다툼을 일으키는 자라

15 Therefore disaster will overtake him in an instant; he will suddenly be destroyed—without remedy.

데어포어 디재스터 윌 오우버테익 힘 인 앤 인스턴트 히 윌 서더늘리 비 디스트로이드 위다우트 레머디.

그러므로 그의 재앙이 갑자기 내려 당장에 멸망하여 살릴 길이 없으리라

16 There are six things the LORD hates, seven that are detestable to him:

데어 아아 식스 씽즈 더 로어드 헤잇스, 세번 댓 아아 디테스터벌 투 힘

여호와께서 미워하시는 것 곧 그의 마음에 싫어하시는 것이 예닐곱 가지이니

17 haughty eyes, a lying tongue, hands that shed innocent blood,

호티 아이즈, 어 라이잉 텅, 핸즈 댓 셰드 이너선트 블러드,

곧 교만한 눈과 거짓된 혀와 무죄한 자의 피를 흘리는 손과

18 a heart that devises wicked schemes, feet that are quick to rush into evil,

어 하아트 댓 디바이지즈 위커드 스킴즈, 핏 댓 아아 퀵 투 러쉬 인투 이벌,

악한 계교를 꾀하는 마음과 빨리 악으로 달려가는 발과

19 a false witness who pours out lies and a person who stirs up conflict in the community.

어 폴스 윗너스 후 포어즈 아웃 라이즈 언드 어 퍼선 후 스터즈 업 칸플릭트 인 더 커뮤너티.
거짓을 말하는 망령된 증인과 및 형제 사이를 이간하는 자이니라

20 My son, keep your father's command and do not forsake your mother's teaching.
마이 선, 킵 요어 파더즈 커맨드 언드 두 낫 포어세익 요어 머더즈 티칭.
내 아들아 네 아비의 명령을 지키며 네 어미의 법을 떠나지 말고

21 Bind them always on your heart; fasten them around your neck.
바인드 뎀 올웨이즈 안 요어 하아트 패선 뎀 어라운드 요어 넥.
그것을 항상 네 마음에 새기며 네 목에 매라

22 When you walk, they will guide you; when you sleep, they will watch over you; when you awake, they will speak to you.
웬 유 웍, 데이 윌 가이드 유 웬 유 슬립, 데이 윌 와치 오우버 유 웬 유 어웨익, 데이 윌 스픽 투 유.
그것이 네가 다닐 때에 너를 인도하며 네가 잘 때에 너를 보호하며 네가 깰 때에 너와 더불어 말하리니

23 For this command is a lamp, this teaching is a light, and correction and instruction are the way to life,
포어 디스 커맨드 이즈 어 램프, 디스 티칭 이즈 어 라이트, 언드 커렉션 언드 인스트럭션 아아 더 웨이 투 라이프.
대저 명령은 등불이요 법은 빛이요 훈계의 책망은 곧 생명의 길이라

24 keeping you from your neighbor's wife, from the smooth talk of a wayward woman.
키핑 유 프럼 요어 네이버즈 와이프, 프럼 더 스뭍 톡 어브 어 웨이워드 워먼.
이것이 너를 지켜 악한 여인에게, 이방 여인의 혀로 호리는 말에 빠지지 않게 하리라

25 Do not lust in your heart after her beauty or let her captivate you with her eyes.
두 낫 러스트 인 요어 하아트 애프터 허 뷰티 오어 렛 허 캡티베이트 유 윋 허 아이즈.
네 마음에 그의 아름다움을 탐하지 말며 그 눈꺼풀에 홀리지 말라

26 For a prostitute can be had for a loaf of bread, but another man's wife preys on your very life.
포어 어 프라스터툿 캔 비 해드 포어 어 로우프 어브 브레드, 벗 어너더 맨즈 와이프 프레이즈 안 요어 베어리 라이프.
음녀로 말미암아 사람이 한 조각 떡만 남게 됨이며 음란한 여인은 귀한 생명을 사냥함이니라

27 Can a man scoop fire into his lap without his clothes being burned?
캔 어 맨 스쿱 파여 인투 히즈 랩 위다우트 히즈 클로욷즈 비잉 번드?
사람이 불을 품에 품고서야 어찌 그의 옷이 타지 아니하겠으며

28 Can a man walk on hot coals without his feet being scorched?
캔 어 맨 웍 안 핫 코울즈 위다우트 히즈 핏 비잉 스코어치트?
사람이 숯불을 밟고서야 어찌 그의 발이 데지 아니하겠느냐

29 So is he who sleeps with another man's wife; no one who touches her will go unpunished.
소우 이즈 히 후 슬립스 윋 어너더 맨즈 와이프 노우 원 후 터처즈 허 윌 고우 언퍼니쉬트.
남의 아내와 통간하는 자도 이와 같을 것이라 그를 만지는 자마다 벌을 면하지 못하리라

30 People do not despise a thief if he steals to satisfy his hunger when he is starving.
피펄 두 낫 디스파이즈 어 씨프 이프 히 스틸즈 투 새터스파이 히즈 헝거 웬 히 이즈 스타아빙.
도둑이 만일 주릴 때에 배를 채우려고 도둑질하면 사람이 그를 멸시하지는 아니하려니와

31 Yet if he is caught, he must pay sevenfold, though it costs him all the wealth of his house.
옛 이프 히 이즈 콧, 히 머스트 페이 세번포울드, 도우 잇 카스트스 힘 올 더 웰쓰 어브 히즈 하우스.

들키면 칠 배를 갚아야 하리니 심지어 자기 집에 있는 것을 다 내주게 되리라

32 But a man who commits adultery has no sense; whoever does so destroys himself.
벗 어 맨 후 커밋스 어덜터리 해즈 노우 센스 후에버 더즈 소우 디스트로이즈 힘셀프.
여인과 간음하는 자는 무지한 자라 이것을 행하는 자는 자기의 영혼을 망하게 하며

33 Blows and disgrace are his lot, and his shame will never be wiped away.
블로우즈 언드 디스그레이스 아아 히즈 랏, 언드 히즈 셰임 윌 네버 비 와입트 어웨이.
상함과 능욕을 받고 부끄러움을 씻을 수 없게 되나니

34 For jealousy arouses a husband's fury, and he will show no mercy when he takes revenge.
포어 젤러시 어아우지즈 어 허즈번즈 퓨리, 언드 히 윌 쇼우 노우 머시 웬 히 테익스 리벤지.
남편이 투기로 분노하여 원수 갚는 날에 용서하지 아니하고

35 He will not accept any compensation; he will refuse a bribe, however great it is.
히 윌 낫 억셉트 에니 캄펀세이션 히 윌 리퓨즈 어 브라이브, 하우에버 그레이트 잇 이즈.
어떤 보상도 받지 아니하며 많은 선물을 줄지라도 듣지 아니하리라

pledge [pledʒ] n. 서약, 언질
trap [træp] n. 올가미, 함정
exhaustion [igzɔ́ːstʃən] n. 소모
slumber [slʌ́mbər] n. 잠, 선잠
eyelid [áilìd] n. 눈꺼풀
sluggard [slʌ́gərd] n. 게으름쟁이
consider [kənsídər] vt. 숙고하다
ruler [rúːlər] n. 통치자, 주권자
provision [prəvíʒən] n. 예비, 준비
harvest [hɑ́ːrvist] n. 수확, 추수
poverty [pɑ́vərti] n. 가난, 빈곤
scarcity [skέərsəti] n. 부족, 기근
villain [vílən] n. 악인, 악역
malicious [məlíʃəs] a. 악의 있는
conflict [kɑ́nflikt] n. 싸움, 다툼
suddenly [sʌ́dnli] ad. 갑자기
remedy [rémədi] n. 치료, 의료
devise [diváiz] vt. 궁리하다
scoop [skuːp] n. 국자, 주걱
scorch [skɔːrtʃ] vt. 그슬리다
steal [stiːl] vt. 훔치다
jealousy [dʒéləsi] n. 질투, 투기
arouse [əráuz] vt. 자극하다
revenge [rivéndʒ] n. 보복, 복수

7장 1 My son, keep my words and store up my commands within you.
마이 선, 킵 마이 워즈 언드 스토어 업 마이 커맨즈 위씬 유.
내 아들아 내 말을 지키며 내 계명을 간직하라

2 Keep my commands and you will live; guard my teachings as the apple of your eye.
킵 마이 커맨즈 언드 유 윌 라이브 가아드 마이 티칭즈 애즈 디 애펄 어브 요어 아이.
내 계명을 지켜 살며 내 법을 네 눈동자처럼 지키라

3 Bind them on your fingers; write them on the tablet of your heart.
바인드 뎀 안 요어 핑거즈 라이트 뎀 안 더 태블럿 어브 요어 하아트.
이것을 네 손가락에 매며 이것을 네 마음판에 새기라

4 Say to wisdom, "You are my sister," and to insight, "You are my relative."
세이 투 위즈덤, 유 아아 마이 시스터, 언드 투 인사이트, 유 아아 마이 렐러티브.
지혜에게 너는 내 누이라 하며 명철에게 너는 내 친족이라 하라

5 They will keep you from the adulterous woman, from the wayward woman with her seductive words.
데이 윌 킵 유 프럼 디 어덜터러스 워먼, 프럼 더 웨이워드 워먼 윋 허 시덕티브 워즈.
그리하면 이것이 너를 지켜서 음녀에게, 말로 호리는 이방 여인에게 빠지지 않게 하리라

6 At the window of my house I looked down through the lattice.
앳 더 윈도우 어브 마이 하우스 아이 룩트 다운 쓰루 더 래터스.

내가 내 집 들창으로, 살창으로 내다 보다가

7 I saw among the simple, I noticed among the young men, a youth who had no sense.
아이 소 어멍 더 심펄, 아이 노우티스트 어멍 더 영 멘, 어 유쓰 후 해드 노우 센스.
어리석은 자 중에, 젊은이 가운데에 한 지혜 없는 자를 보았노라

8 He was going down the street near her corner, walking along in the direction of her house
히 와즈 고우잉 다운 더 스트릿 니어 허 코어너, 워킹 얼롱 인 더 더렉션 어브 허 하우스
그가 거리를 지나 음녀의 골목 모퉁이로 가까이 하여 그의 집쪽으로 가는데

9 at twilight, as the day was fading, as the dark of night set in.
앳 트와이라이트, 애즈 더 데이 와즈 페이딩, 애즈 더 다아크 어브 나이트 셋 인.
저물 때, 황혼 때, 깊은 밤 흑암 중에라

10 Then out came a woman to meet him, dressed like a prostitute and with crafty intent.
덴 아웃 케임 어 워먼 투 밋 힘, 드레스트 라익 어 프라스터툿 언드 윋 크래프티 인텐트.
그 때에 기생의 옷을 입은 간교한 여인이 그를 맞으니

11 (She is unruly and defiant, her feet never stay at home;
쉬 이즈 언룰리 언드 디파이언트, 허 핏 네버 스테이 앳 호움
이 여인은 떠들며 완악하며 그의 발이 집에 머물지 아니하여

12 now in the street, now in the squares, at every corner she lurks.)
나우 인 더 스트릿, 나우 인 더 스퀘즈, 앳 에브리 코어너 쉬 럭스.
어떤 때에는 거리, 어떤 때에는 광장 또 모퉁이마다 서서 사람을 기다리는 자라

13 She took hold of him and kissed him and with a brazen face she said:
쉬 툭 호울드 어브 힘 언드 키스트 힘 언드 윋 어 브레이전 페이스 쉬 세드
그 여인이 그를 붙잡고 그에게 입맞추며 부끄러움을 모르는 얼굴로 그에게 말하되

14 "Today I fulfilled my vows, and I have food from my fellowship offering at home.
터데이 아이 풀필드 마이 바우즈, 언드 아이 해브 푸드 프럼 마이 펠로우쉽 오퍼링 앳 호움.
내가 화목제를 드려 서원한 것을 오늘 갚았노라

15 So I came out to meet you; I looked for you and have found you!
소우 아이 케임 아웃 투 밋 유 아이 룩트 포어 유 언드 해브 파운드 유!
이러므로 내가 너를 맞으려고 나와 네 얼굴을 찾다가 너를 만났도다

16 I have covered my bed with colored linens from Egypt.
아이 해브 커버드 마이 베드 윋 컬러드 리넌즈 프럼 이접트.
내 침상에는 요와 애굽의 무늬 있는 이불을 폈고

17 I have perfumed my bed with myrrh, aloes and cinnamon.
아이 해브 퍼퓸드 마이 베드 윋 머, 앨로우즈 언드 시너먼.
몰약과 침향과 계피를 뿌렸노라

18 Come, let's drink deeply of love till morning; let's enjoy ourselves with love!
컴, 렛스 드링크 디플리 어브 러브 틸 모어닝 렛스 엔조이 아우어셀브즈 윋 러브!
오라 우리가 아침까지 흡족하게 서로 사랑하며 사랑함으로 희락하자

19 My husband is not at home; he has gone on a long journey.

마이 허즈번드 이즈 낫 앳 호움 히 해즈 곤 안 어 롱 저니.
남편은 집을 떠나 먼 길을 갔는데

20 He took his purse filled with money and will not be home till full moon."
히 툭 히즈 퍼스 필드 윋 머니 언드 윌 낫 비 호움 틸 풀 문.
은 주머니를 가졌은즉 보름 날에나 집에 돌아오리라 하여

21 With persuasive words she led him astray; she seduced him with her smooth talk.
윋 퍼쉐시브 워즈 쉬 레드 힘 어스트레이 쉬 시두스트 힘 윋 허 스묻 톡.
여러 가지 고운 말로 유혹하며 입술의 호리는 말로 꾀므로

22 All at once he followed her like an ox going to the slaughter, like a deer stepping into a noose
올 앳 원스 히 팔로우드 허 라익 앤 악스 고우잉 투 더 슬로터, 라익 어 디어 스테핑 인투 어 누스
젊은이가 곧 그를 따랐으니 소가 도수장으로 가는 것 같고 미련한 자가 벌을 받으려고 쇠사슬에 매이러 가는 것과 같도다

23 till an arrow pierces his liver, like a bird darting into a snare, little knowing it will cost him his life.
틸 앤 애어로우 피어시즈 히즈 리버, 라익 어 버드 다아팅 인투 어 스네어, 리털 노우잉 잇 윌 카스트 힘 히즈 라이프.
필경은 화살이 그 간을 뚫게 되리라 새가 빨리 그물로 들어가되 그의 생명을 잃어버릴 줄을 알지 못함과 같으니라

24 Now then, my sons, listen to me; pay attention to what I say.
나우 덴, 마이 선즈, 리선 투 미 페이 어텐션 투 윗 아이 세이.
이제 아들들아 내 말을 듣고 내 입의 말에 주의하라

25 Do not let your heart turn to her ways or stray into her paths.
두 낫 렛 요어 하아트 턴 투 허 웨이즈 오어 스트레이 인투 허 팬즈.
네 마음이 음녀의 길로 치우치지 말며 그 길에 미혹되지 말지어다

26 Many are the victims she has brought down; her slain are a mighty throng.
메니 아아 더 빅팀즈 쉬 해즈 브롯 다운 허 슬레인 아아 어 마이티 쓰롱.
대저 그가 많은 사람을 상하여 엎드러지게 하였나니 그에게 죽은 자가 허다하니라

27 Her house is a highway to the grave, leading down to the chambers of death.
허 하우스 이즈 어 하이웨이 투 더 그레이브, 리딩 다운 투 더 체임버즈 어브 데쓰.
그의 집은 스올의 길이라 사망의 방으로 내려가느니라

tablet [tǽblit] n. 평판, 명판
relative [rélətiv] a. 비교상의
lattice [lǽtis] n. 격자
street [striːt] n. 거리, 가로
sense [sens] n. 분별력, 센스
corner [kɔ́ːrnər] n. 모퉁이
twilight [twáilàit] n. 황혼
crafty [krǽfti] a. 교활한
unruly [ʌnrúːli] a. 사나운
defiant [difáiənt] a. 반항적인
lurk [ləːrk] vi. 잠복하다
brazen [bréizən] a. 놋쇠로 만든
fellowship [félouʃip] n. 친구, 동료
offering [ɔ́(ː)fəriŋ] n. 공물, 제물
perfume [pə́ːrfjuːm] n. 향기, 향료
myrrh [məːr] n. 몰약
cinnamon [sínəmən] n. 계피
journey [dʒə́ːrni] n. 여행
seduce [sidjúːs] vt. 부추기다
smooth [smuːð] a. 매끄러운
slaughter [slɔ́ːtər] n. 도살
noose [nuːs] n. 올가미
victim [víktim] n. 희생(자)
chamber [tʃéimbər] n. 방, 침실

8장 1 Does not wisdom call out? Does not understanding raise her voice?
더즈 낫 위즈덤 콜 아웃? 더즈 낫 언더스탠딩 레이즈 허 보이스?
지혜가 부르지 아니하느냐 명철이 소리를 높이지 아니하느냐

2 At the highest point along the way, where the paths meet, she takes her stand;
앳 더 하이어스트 포인트 얼롱 더 웨이, 웨어 더 팬즈 밋, 쉬 테익스 허 스탠드
그가 길 가의 높은 곳과 네거리에 서며

3 beside the gate leading into the city, at the entrance, she cries aloud:
비사이드 더 게이트 리딩 인투 더 시티, 앳 디 엔트런스, 쉬 크라이즈 얼라우드
성문 곁과 문 어귀와 여러 출입하는 문에서 불러 이르되

4 "To you, O people, I call out; I raise my voice to all mankind.
투 유, 오우 피펄, 아이 콜 아웃 아이 레이즈 마이 보이스 투 올 맨카인드
사람들아 내가 너희를 부르며 내가 인자들에게 소리를 높이노라

5 You who are simple, gain prudence; you who are foolish, set your hearts on it.
유 후 아아 심펄, 게인 프루던스 유 후 아아 풀리쉬, 셋 요어 하아트스 안 잇.
어리석은 자들아 너희는 명철할지니라 미련한 자들아 너희는 마음이 밝을지니라

6 Listen, for I have trustworthy things to say; I open my lips to speak what is right.
리선, 포어 아이 해브 트러스트워디 씽즈 투 세이 아이 오우펀 마이 립스 투 스픽 윗 이즈 나이트.
너희는 들을지어다 내가 가장 선한 것을 말하리라 내 입술을 열어 정직을 내리라

7 My mouth speaks what is true, for my lips detest wickedness.
마이 마우쓰 스픽스 윗 이즈 트루, 포어 마이 립스 디테스트 위커드너스.
내 입은 진리를 말하며 내 입술은 악을 미워하느니라

8 All the words of my mouth are just; none of them is crooked or perverse.
올 더 워즈 어브 마이 마우쓰 아아 저스트 넌 어브 뎀 이즈 크루커드 오어 퍼버스.
내 입의 말은 다 의로운즉 그 가운데에 굽은 것과 패역한 것이 없나니

9 To the discerning all of them are right; they are upright to those who have found knowledge.
투 더 디서닝 올 어브 뎀 아아 라이트 데이 아아 업라이트 투 도우즈 후 해브 파운드 날러지.
이는 다 총명 있는 자가 밝히 아는 바요 지식 얻은 자가 정직하게 여기는 바니라

10 Choose my instruction instead of silver, knowledge rather than choice gold,
추즈 마이 인스트럭션 인스테드 어브 실버, 날러지 래더 던 초이스 고울드,
너희가 은을 받지 말고 나의 훈계를 받으며 정금보다 지식을 얻으라

11 for wisdom is more precious than rubies, and nothing you desire can compare with her.
포어 위즈덤 이즈 모어 프레셔스 던 루비즈, 언드 너씽 유 디자여 캔 컴페어 윋 허.
대저 지혜는 진주보다 나으므로 원하는 모든 것을 이에 비교할 수 없음이니라

12 "I, wisdom, dwell together with prudence; I possess knowledge and discretion.
아이, 위즈덤, 웰 터게더 윋 프루던스 아이 퍼제스 날러지 언드 디스크레션.
나 지혜는 명철로 주소를 삼으며 지식과 근신을 찾아 얻나니

13 To fear the LORD is to hate evil; I hate pride and arrogance, evil behavior and perverse speech.
투 피어 더 로어드 이즈 투 헤이트 이벌 아이 헤이트 프라이드 언드 에어러건스, 이벌 비헤이브여 언드 퍼버스 스피치.
여호와를 경외하는 것은 악을 미워하는 것이라 나는 교만과 거만과 악한 행실과 패역한 입을 미워하느니라

14 Counsel and sound judgment are mine; I have insight, I have power.
카운설 언드 사운드 저지먼트 아아 마인 아이 해브 인사이트, 아이 해브 파워.

내게는 계략과 참 지식이 있으며 나는 명철이라 내게 능력이 있으므로

15 By me kings reign and rulers issue decrees that are just;
바이 미 킹즈 레인 언드 룰러즈 이슈 디크리즈 댓 아아 저스트
나로 말미암아 왕들이 치리하며 방백들이 공의를 세우며

16 by me princes govern, and nobles—all who rule on earth.
바이 미 프린서즈 거번, 언드 노우벌즈 올 후 룰 안 어쓰.
나로 말미암아 재상과 존귀한 자 곧 모든 의로운 재판관들이 다스리느니라

17 I love those who love me, and those who seek me find me.
아이 러브 도우즈 후 러브 미, 언드 도우즈 후 식 미 파인드 미.
나를 사랑하는 자들이 나의 사랑을 입으며 나를 간절히 찾는 자가 나를 만날 것이니라

18 With me are riches and honor, enduring wealth and prosperity.
윋 미 아아 리처즈 언드 아너, 엔듀링 웰쓰 언드 프라스페러티.
부귀가 내게 있고 장구한 재물과 공의도 그러하니라

19 My fruit is better than fine gold; what I yield surpasses choice silver.
마이 프룻 이즈 베터 던 파인 고울드 윗 아이 일드 서패시즈 초이스 실버.
내 열매는 금이나 정금보다 나으며 내 소득은 순은보다 나으니라

20 I walk in the way of righteousness, along the paths of justice,
아이 웍 인 더 웨이 어브 라이처스너스, 얼롱 더 팯즈 어브 저스터스.
나는 정의로운 길로 행하며 공의로운 길 가운데로 다니나니

21 bestowing a rich inheritance on those who love me and making their treasuries full.
비스토우잉 어 리치 인헤러턴스 안 도우즈 후 러브 미 언드 메이킹 데어 트레저리즈 풀.
이는 나를 사랑하는 자가 재물을 얻어서 그 곳간에 채우게 하려 함이니라

22 "The LORD brought me forth as the first of his works, before his deeds of old;
더 로어드 브롯 미 포어쓰 애즈 더 퍼스트 어브 히즈 웍스, 비포어 히즈 디즈 어브 오울드
여호와께서 그 조화의 시작 곧 태초에 일하시기 전에 나를 가지셨으며

23 I was formed long ages ago, at the very beginning, when the world came to be.
아이 와즈 폼드 롱 에이지즈 어고우, 앳 더 베어리 비기닝, 웬 더 월드 케임 투 비이
만세 전부터, 태초부터, 땅이 생기기 전부터 내가 세움을 받았나니

24 When there were no watery depths, I was given birth, when there were no springs overflowing with water;
웬 데어 워 노우 워터리 뎁쓰스, 아이 와즈 기번 버쓰, 웬 데어 워 노우 스프링즈 오우버플로우잉 윋 워터
아직 바다가 생기지 아니하였고 큰 샘들이 있기 전에 내가 이미 났으며

25 before the mountains were settled in place, before the hills, I was given birth,
비포어 더 마운턴즈 워 세털드 인 플레이스, 비포어 더 힐즈, 아이 와즈 기번 버쓰,
산이 세워지기 전에, 언덕이 생기기 전에 내가 이미 났으니

26 before he made the world or its fields or any of the dust of the earth.
비포어 히 메이드 더 월드 오어 잇스 필즈 오어 에니 어브 더 더스트 어브 디 어쓰.
하나님이 아직 땅도, 들도, 세상 진토의 근원도 짓지 아니하셨을 때에라

27 I was there when he set the heavens in place, when he marked out the horizon on the face of the deep,

아이 와즈 데어 웬 히 셋 더 헤번즈 인 플레이스, 웬 히 마아크트 아웃 더 허라이전 안 더 페이스 어브 더 딥,
그가 하늘을 지으시며 궁창을 해면에 두르실 때에 내가 거기 있었고

28 when he established the clouds above and fixed securely the fountains of the deep,
웬 히 이스태블리쉬트 더 클라우즈 어버브 언드 픽스트 시큐리 더 파운턴즈 어브 더 딥,
그가 위로 구름 하늘을 견고하게 하시며 바다의 샘들을 힘 있게 하시며

29 when he gave the sea its boundary so the waters would not overstep his command, and when he marked out the foundations of the earth.
웬 히 게이브 더 시 잇스 바운더리 소우 더 워터즈 워드 낫 오우버스텝 히즈 커맨드, 언드 웬 히 마아크트 아웃 더 파운데이션즈 어브 디 어쓰
바다의 한계를 정하여 물이 명령을 거스르지 못하게 하시며 또 땅의 기초를 정하실 때에

30 Then I was the constantly at his side. I was filled with delight day after day, rejoicing always in his presence,
덴 아이 와즈 더 칸스턴틀리 앳 히즈 사이드 아이 와즈 필드 윋 딜랏 데이 애프터 데이, 리조이싱 올웨이즈 인 히즈 프레전스,
내가 그 곁에 있어서 창조자가 되어 날마다 그의 기뻐하신 바가 되었으며 항상 그 앞에서 즐거워하였으며

31 rejoicing in his whole world and delighting in mankind.
리조이싱 인 히즈 호울 월드 언드 딜라이팅 인 맨카인드.
사람이 거처할 땅에서 즐거워하며 인자들을 기뻐하였느니라

32 "Now then, my children, listen to me; blessed are those who keep my ways.
나우 덴, 마이 칠드런, 리선 투 미 블레스트 아아 도우즈 후 킵 마이 웨이즈.
아들들아 이제 내게 들으라 내 도를 지키는 자가 복이 있느니라

33 Listen to my instruction and be wise; do not disregard it.
리선 투 마이 인스트럭션 언드 비 와이즈 두 낫 디스리가아드 잇.
훈계를 들어서 지혜를 얻으라 그것을 버리지 말라

34 Blessed are those who listen to me, watching daily at my doors, waiting at my doorway.
블레스트 아아 도우즈 후 리선 투 미, 와칭 데일리 앳 마이 도어즈, 웨이팅 앳 마이 도어루에이.
누구든지 내게 들으며 날마다 내 문 곁에서 기다리며 문설주 옆에서 기다리는 자는 복이 있나니

35 For those who find me find life and receive favor from the LORD.
포어 도우즈 후 파인드 미 파인드 라이프 언드 러시브 페이버 프럼 더 로어드.
대저 나를 얻는 자는 생명을 얻고 여호와께 은총을 얻을 것임이니라

36 But those who fail to find me harm themselves; all who hate me love death.
벗 도우즈 후 페일 투 파인드 미 함 뎀셀브즈 올 후 헤이트 미 러브 데쓰.
그러나 나를 잃는 자는 자기의 영혼을 해하는 자라 나를 미워하는 자는 사망을 사랑하느니라

raise [reiz] vt. 올리다	instead [instéd] ad. 그 대신에	govern [gʌ́vərn] vt. 통치하다
voice [vɔis] n. 목소리	desire [dizáiər] vt. 바라다, 원하다	surpass [sərpǽs] vt. 뛰어나다
highest [háiist] a. 가장 높은	compare [kəmpέər] vt. 비교하다	inheritance [inhéritəns] n. 상속
beside [bisáid] prep. …의 곁에	dwell [dwel] vi. 거주하다	depth [depθ] n. 깊이, 깊음
entrance [éntrəns] n. 입구	arrogance [ǽrəgəns] n. 오만	horizon [həráizən] n. 수평선
aloud [əláud] ad. 큰 소리로	judgment [dʒʌ́dʒmənt] n. 재판	establish [istǽbliʃ] vt. 설립하다
trustworthy [trʌ́stwə̀ːrðì] a. 확실한	issue [íʃuːː] vt. 발포하다	boundary [báundəri] n. 경계(선)

detest [ditést] vt. 혐오하다 decree [dikríː] n. 법령, 포고 disregard [dìsrigάːrd] vt. 무시하다

9장 1 Wisdom has built her house; she has set up its seven pillars.
위즈덤 해즈 빌트 허 하우스 쉬 해즈 셋 업 잇스 세번 필러즈.
지혜가 그의 집을 짓고 일곱 기둥을 다듬고

2 She has prepared her meat and mixed her wine; she has also set her table.
쉬 해즈 프리페어드 허 밋 언드 믹스트 허 와인 쉬 해즈 올소우 셋 허 테이벌.
짐승을 잡으며 포도주를 혼합하여 상을 갖추고

3 She has sent out her servants, and she calls from the highest point of the city,
쉬 해즈 센트 아웃 허 서번트스, 언드 쉬 콜즈 프럼 더 하이어스트 포인트 어브 더 시티.
자기의 여종을 보내어 성중 높은 곳에서 불러 이르기를

4 "Let all who are simple come to my house!" To those who have no sense she says,
렛 올 후 아아 심펄 컴 투 마이 하우스! 투 도우즈 후 해브 노우 센스 쉬 세즈.
어리석은 자는 이리로 돌이키라 또 지혜 없는 자에게 이르기를

5 "Come, eat my food and drink the wine I have mixed.
컴, 잇 마이 푸드 언드 드링크 더 와인 아이 해브 믹스트.
너는 와서 내 식물을 먹으며 내 혼합한 포도주를 마시고

6 Leave your simple ways and you will live; walk in the way of insight."
리브 요어 심펄 웨이즈 언드 유 윌 라이브 웍 인 더 웨이 어브 인사이트.
어리석음을 버리고 생명을 얻으라 명철의 길을 행하라 하느니라

7 Whoever corrects a mocker invites insults; whoever rebukes the wicked incurs abuse.
후에버 커렉트스 어 마커 인바잇스 인설트스 후에버 리북스 더 위커드 인커즈 어뷰스.
거만한 자를 징계하는 자는 도리어 능욕을 받고 악인을 책망하는 자는 도리어 흠이 잡히느니라

8 Do not rebuke mockers or they will hate you; rebuke the wise and they will love you.
두 낫 리북 마커즈 오어 데이 윌 헤이트 유 리북 더 와이즈 언드 데이 윌 러브 유.
거만한 자를 책망하지 말라 그가 너를 미워할까 두려우니라 지혜 있는 자를 책망하라 그가 너를 사랑하리라

9 Instruct the wise and they will be wiser still; teach the righteous and they will add to their learning.
인스트럭트 더 와이즈 언드 데이 윌 비 와이저 스틸 티치 더 라이처스 언드 데이 윌 애드 투 데어 러닝.
지혜 있는 자에게 교훈을 더하라 그가 더욱 지혜로워질 것이요 의로운 사람을 가르치라 그의 학식이 더하리라

10 The fear of the LORD is the beginning of wisdom, and knowledge of the Holy One is understanding.
더 피어 어브 더 로어드 이즈 더 비기닝 어브 위즈덤, 언드 날러지 어브 더 호울리 원 이즈 언더스탠딩.
여호와를 경외하는 것이 지혜의 근본이요 거룩하신 자를 아는 것이 명철이니라

11 For through wisdom your days will be many, and years will be added to your life.
포어 쓰루 위즈덤 요어 데이즈 윌 비 메니, 언드 이어즈 윌 비 애디드 투 요어 라이프.
나 지혜로 말미암아 네 날이 많아질 것이요 네 생명의 해가 네게 더하리라

12 If you are wise, your wisdom will reward you; if you are a mocker, you alone will suffer.
이프 유 아아 와이즈, 요어 위즈덤 윌 리워어드 유 이프 유 아아 어 마커, 유 얼로운 윌 서퍼.

네가 만일 지혜로우면 그 지혜가 네게 유익할 것이나 네가 만일 거만하면 너 홀로 해를 당하리라

13 Folly is an unruly woman; she is simple and knows nothing.
팔리 이즈 앤 언룰리 워먼 쉬 이즈 심펄 언드 노우즈 너씽.
미련한 여인이 떠들며 어리석어서 아무것도 알지 못하고

14 She sits at the door of her house, on a seat at the highest point of the city,
쉬 싯스 앳 더 도어 어브 허 하우스, 안 어 싯 앳 더 하이어스트 포인트 어브 더 시티.
자기 집 문에 앉으며 성읍 높은 곳에 있는 자리에 앉아서

15 calling out to those who pass by, who go straight on their way,
콜링 아웃 투 도우즈 후 패스 바이, 후 고우 스트레이트 안 데어 웨이.
자기 길을 바로 가는 행인들을 불러 이르되

16 "Let all who are simple come to my house!" To those who have no sense she says,
렛 올 후 아아 심펄 컴 투 마이 하우스! 투 도우즈 후 해브 노우 센스 쉬 세즈.
어리석은 자는 이리로 돌이키라 또 지혜 없는 자에게 이르기를

17 "Stolen water is sweet; food eaten in secret is delicious!"
스토울런 워터 이즈 스윗 푸드 이턴 인 시크럿 이즈 딜리셔스!
도둑질한 물이 달고 몰래 먹는 떡이 맛이 있다 하는도다

18 But little do they know that the dead are there, that her guests are deep in the realm of the dead.
벗 리털 두 데이 노우 댓 더 데드 아아 데어, 댓 허 게스트스 아아 딥 인 더 렐므 어브 더 데드.
오직 그 어리석은 자는 죽은 자들이 거기 있는 것과 그의 객들이 스올 깊은 곳에 있는 것을 알지 못하느니라

built [bilt] a. 조립식의
pillar [pílər] n. 기둥
prepare [pripέər] vt. 준비하다
mixed [mikst] a. 섞인
wine [wain] n. 포도주
servant [sə́:rvənt] n. 하인
call [kɔ:l] vt. 부르다
point [pɔint] n. 뾰족한 끝
correct [kərékt] a. 정확한
invite [inváit] vt. 초청하다
insult [ínsʌlt] n. 모욕, 무례
abuse [əbjú:z] vt. 남용하다
rebuke [ribjú:k] vt. 꾸짖다
still [stil] ad. 여전히
add [æd] vt. 더하다
learn [lə:rn] vt. …을 배우다
reward [riwɔ́:rd] n. 보수, 포상
suffer [sʌ́fər] vi. 괴로워하다
seat [si:t] n. 자리, 좌석
folly [fɑ́li] n. 어리석음, 우둔
delicious [dilíʃəs] a. 맛있는
guest [gest] n. 손(님), 객
realm [relm] n. 왕국, 국토
dead [ded] a. 죽은

10장 1 The proverbs of Solomon: A wise son brings joy to his father, but a foolish son brings grief to his mother.
더 프라버브즈 어브 살러먼 어 와이즈 선 브링즈 조이 투 히즈 파더, 벗 어 풀리쉬 선 브링즈 그리프 투 히즈 머더.
솔로몬의 잠언이라 지혜로운 아들은 아비를 기쁘게 하거니와 미련한 아들은 어미의 근심이니라

2 Ill-gotten treasures have no lasting value, but righteousness delivers from death.
일가턴 트레저즈 해브 노우 래스팅 밸류, 벗 라이처스너스 딜리버즈 프럼 데쓰.
불의의 재물은 무익하여도 공의는 죽음에서 건지느니라

3 The LORD does not let the righteous go hungry, but he thwarts the craving of the wicked.
더 로어드 더즈 낫 렛 더 라이처스 고우 헝그리, 벗 히 쒈트스 더 크레이빙 어브 더 위커드.
여호와께서 의인의 영혼은 주리지 않게 하시나 악인의 소욕은 물리치시느니라

4 Lazy hands make for poverty, but diligent hands bring wealth.

레이지 핸즈 메익 포어 파버티, 벗 딜리전트 핸즈 브링 웰쓰.
손을 게으르게 놀리는 자는 가난하게 되고 손이 부지런한 자는 부하게 되느니라

5 He who gathers crops in summer is a prudent son, but he who sleeps during harvest is a disgraceful son.
히 후 개더즈 크랍스 인 서머 이즈 어 프루던트 선, 벗 히 후 슬립스 두링 하아버스트 이즈 어 디스그레이스펄 선.
여름에 거두는 자는 지혜로운 아들이나 추수 때에 자는 자는 부끄러움을 끼치는 아들이니라

6 Blessings crown the head of the righteous, but violence overwhelms the mouth of the wicked.
블레싱즈 크라운 더 헤드 어브 더 라이처스, 벗 바이얼런스 오우버웰므즈 더 마우쓰 어브 더 위커드.
의인의 머리에는 복이 임하나 악인의 입은 독을 머금었느니라

7 The name of the righteous is used in blessings, but the name of the wicked will rot.
더 네임 어브 더 라이처스 이즈 유즈드 인 블레싱즈, 벗 더 네임 어브 더 위커드 윌 랏.
의인을 기념할 때에는 칭찬하거니와 악인의 이름은 썩게 되느니라

8 The wise in heart accept commands, but a chattering fool comes to ruin.
더 와이즈 인 하아트 억셉트 커맨즈, 벗 어 채터링 풀 컴즈 투 루언.
마음이 지혜로운 자는 계명을 받거니와 입이 미련한 자는 멸망하리라

9 Whoever walks in integrity walks securely, but whoever takes crooked paths will be found out.
후에버 웍스 인 인테그러티 웍스 시큐리, 벗 후에버 테익스 크루커드 팯즈 윌 비 파운드 아웃.
바른 길로 행하는 자는 걸음이 평안하려니와 굽은 길로 행하는 자는 드러나리라

10 Whoever winks maliciously causes grief, and a chattering fool comes to ruin.
후에버 윙크스 멀리쉬슬리 카저즈 그리프, 언드 어 채터링 풀 컴즈 투 루언.
눈짓하는 자는 근심을 끼치고 입이 미련한 자는 멸망하느니라

11 The mouth of the righteous is a fountain of life, but the mouth of the wicked conceals violence.
더 마우쓰 어브 더 라이처스 이즈 어 파운턴 어브 라이프, 벗 더 마우쓰 어브 더 위커드 컨실즈 바이얼런스.
의인의 입은 생명의 샘이라도 악인의 입은 독을 머금었느니라

12 Hatred stirs up conflict, but love covers over all wrongs.
헤잇러드 스터즈 업 칸플릭트, 벗 러브 커버즈 오우버 올 롱즈.
미움은 다툼을 일으켜도 사랑은 모든 허물을 가리느니라

13 Wisdom is found on the lips of the discerning, but a rod is for the back of one who has no sense.
위즈덤 이즈 파운드 안 더 립스 어브 더 디서닝, 벗 어 라드 이즈 포어 더 백 어브 원 후 해즈 노우 센스.
명철한 자의 입술에는 지혜가 있어도 지혜 없는 자의 등을 위하여는 채찍이 있느니라

14 The wise store up knowledge, but the mouth of a fool invites ruin.
더 와이즈 스토어 업 날러지, 벗 더 마우쓰 어브 어 풀 인바잇스 루언.
지혜로운 자는 지식을 간직하거니와 미련한 자의 입은 멸망에 가까우니라

15 The wealth of the rich is their fortified city, but poverty is the ruin of the poor.
더 웰쓰 어브 더 리치 이즈 데어 포어터파이드 시티, 벗 파버티 이즈 더 루언 어브 더 푸어.
부자의 재물은 그의 견고한 성이요 가난한 자의 궁핍은 그의 멸망이니라

16 The wages of the righteous is life, but the earnings of the wicked are sin and death.
더 웨이저즈 어브 더 라이처스 이즈 라이프, 벗 디 어닝즈 어브 더 위커드 아아 신 언드 데쓰.
의인의 수고는 생명에 이르고 악인의 소득은 죄에 이르느니라

17 Whoever heeds discipline shows the way to life, but whoever ignores correction leads others astray.
후에버 히즈 디서플런 쇼우즈 더 웨이 투 라이프, 벗 후에버 이그노어즈 커렉션 리즈 어더즈 어스트레이.
훈계를 지키는 자는 생명 길로 행하여도 징계를 버리는 자는 그릇 가느니라

18 Whoever conceals hatred with lying lips and spreads slander is a fool.
후에버 컨실즈 헤잇러드 윋 라이잉 립스 언드 스프레즈 슬랜더 이즈 어 풀.
미움을 감추는 자는 거짓된 입술을 가진 자요 중상하는 자는 미련한 자이니라

19 Sin is not ended by multiplying words, but the prudent hold their tongues.
신 이즈 낫 엔더드 바이 멀터플라이잉 워즈, 벗 더 프루던트 호울드 데어 텅즈.
말이 많으면 허물을 면하기 어려우나 그 입술을 제어하는 자는 지혜가 있느니라

20 The tongue of the righteous is choice silver, but the heart of the wicked is of little value.
더 텅 어브 더 라이처스 이즈 초이스 실버, 벗 더 하아트 어브 더 위커드 이즈 어브 리털 밸류.
의인의 혀는 순은과 같거니와 악인의 마음은 가치가 적으니라

21 The lips of the righteous nourish many, but fools die for lack of sense.
더 립스 어브 더 라이처스 너리쉬 메니, 벗 풀즈 다이 포어 랙 어브 센스.
의인의 입술은 여러 사람을 교육하나 미련한 자는 지식이 없어 죽느니라

22 The blessing of the LORD brings wealth, without painful toil for it.
더 블레싱 어브 더 로어드 브링즈 웰쓰, 위다우트 페인펄 토일 포어 잇.
여호와께서 주시는 복은 사람을 부하게 하고 근심을 겸하여 주지 아니하시느니라

23 A fool finds pleasure in wicked schemes, but a person of understanding delights in wisdom.
어 풀 파인즈 플레저 인 위커드 스킴즈, 벗 어 퍼선 어브 언더스탠딩 딜랏스 인 위즈덤.
미련한 자는 행악으로 낙을 삼는 것 같이 명철한 자는 지혜로 낙을 삼느니라

24 What the wicked dread will overtake them; what the righteous desire will be granted.
웟 더 위커드 드레드 윌 오우버테익 뎀 웟 더 라이처스 디자여 윌 비 그랜터드.
악인에게는 그의 두려워하는 것이 임하거니와 의인은 그 원하는 것이 이루어지느니라

25 When the storm has swept by, the wicked are gone, but the righteous stand firm forever.
웬 더 스톰 해즈 스웹트 바이, 더 위커드 아아 곤, 벗 더 라이처스 스탠드 펌 퍼레버.
회오리바람이 지나가면 악인은 없어져도 의인은 영원한 기초 같으니라

26 As vinegar to the teeth and smoke to the eyes, so are sluggards to those who send them.
애즈 비너거 투 더 티쓰 언드 스모욱 투 디 아이즈, 소우 아아 슬러거즈 투 도우즈 후 센드 뎀.
게으른 자는 그 부리는 사람에게 마치 이에 식초 같고 눈에 연기 같으니라

27 The fear of the LORD adds length to life, but the years of the wicked are cut short.
더 피어 어브 더 로어드 애즈 렝크쓰 투 라이프, 벗 더 이어즈 어브 더 위커드 아아 컷 쇼어트.
여호와를 경외하면 장수하느니라 그러나 악인의 수명은 짧아지느니라

28 The prospect of the righteous is joy, but the hopes of the wicked come to nothing.
더 프라스펙트 어브 더 라이처스 이즈 조이, 벗 더 호웁스 어브 더 위커드 컴 투 너씽.
의인의 소망은 즐거움을 이루어도 악인의 소망은 끊어지느니라

29 The way of the LORD is a refuge for the blameless, but it is the ruin of those who do evil.
더 웨이 어브 더 로어드 이즈 어 레퓨지 포어 더 블레임러스, 벗 잇 이즈 더 루언 어브 도우즈 후 두 이벌.

여호와의 도가 정직한 자에게는 산성이요 행악하는 자에게는 멸망이니라

30 The righteous will never be uprooted, but the wicked will not remain in the land.
더 라이처스 윌 네버 비 업루티드, 벗 더 위커드 윌 낫 리메인 인 더 랜드.
의인은 영영히 이동되지 아니하여도 악인은 땅에 거하지 못하게 되느니라

31 From the mouth of the righteous comes the fruit of wisdom, but a perverse tongue will be silenced.
프럼 더 마우쓰 어브 더 라이처스 컴즈 더 프룻 어브 위즈덤, 벗 어 퍼버스 텅 윌 비 사일런스트.
의인의 입은 지혜를 내어도 패역한 혀는 베임을 당할 것이니라

32 The lips of the righteous know what finds favor, but the mouth of the wicked only what is perverse.
더 립스 어브 더 라이처스 노우 웟 파인즈 페이버, 벗 더 마우쓰 어브 더 위커드 오운리 웟 이즈 퍼버스.
의인의 입술은 기쁘게 할 것을 알거늘 악인의 입은 패역을 말하느니라

son [sʌn] n. 아들, 자식	craving [kréiviŋ] n. 갈망, 열망	hatred [héitrid] n. 증오, 원한
bring [briŋ] vt. 가져 오다	diligent [dílədʒənt] a. 근면한	ruin [rúːin] n. 파멸; 파산
joy [dʒɔi] n. 기쁨, 환희	rot [rɑt] n. 썩음, 부패	multiply [mʌ́ltəplài] vt. 늘리다
grief [griːf] n. 슬픔, 비탄	chatter [tʃǽtər] vi. 재잘거리다	slander [slǽndər] n. 중상, 비방
treasure [tréʒər] n. 보배, 재보	integrity [intégrəti] n. 성실	tongue [tʌŋ] n. 혀
value [vǽljuː] n. 가치, 유용성	fountain [fáuntin] n. 분수	overtake [òuvərtéik] vt. 추월하다
deliver [dilívər] vt. 인도하다	conceal [kənsíːl] vt. 숨기다	vinegar [vínigər] n. (식)초
thwart [θwɔːrt] vt. 훼방 놓다	cover [kʌ́vər] vt. 덮다	firm [fəːrm] a. 굳은, 단단한

11장 1 The LORD detests dishonest scales, but accurate weights find favor with him.
더 로어드 디테스트스 디사너스트 스케일즈, 벗 애크여엇 웨잇스 파인드 페이버 윋 힘.
속이는 저울은 여호와께서 미워하시나 공평한 추는 그가 기뻐하시느니라

2 When pride comes, then comes disgrace, but with humility comes wisdom.
웬 프라이드 컴즈, 덴 컴즈 디스그레이스, 벗 윋 휴밀리티 컴즈 위즈덤.
교만이 오면 욕도 오거니와 겸손한 자에게는 지혜가 있느니라

3 The integrity of the upright guides them, but the unfaithful are destroyed by their duplicity.
디 인테그러티 어브 디 업라이트 가이즈 뎀, 벗 디 언페이쓰펄 아아 디스트로이드 바이 데어 두플리시티.
정직한 자의 성실은 자기를 인도하거니와 사악한 자의 패역은 자기를 망하게 하느니라

4 Wealth is worthless in the day of wrath, but righteousness delivers from death.
웰쓰 이즈 워쓸러스 인 더 데이 어브 래쓰, 벗 라이처스너스 딜리버즈 프럼 데쓰.
재물은 진노하시는 날에 무익하나 공의는 죽음에서 건지느니라

5 The righteousness of the blameless makes their paths straight, but the wicked are brought down by their own wickedness.
더 라이처스너스 어브 더 블레임러스 메익스 데어 팯즈 스트레이트, 벗 더 위커드 아아 브롯 다운 바이 데어 오운 위커드너스.
완전한 자의 공의는 자기의 길을 곧게 하려니와 악한 자는 자기의 악으로 말미암아 넘어지리라

6 The righteousness of the upright delivers them, but the unfaithful are trapped by evil desires.

더 라이처스너스 어브 디 업라이트 딜리버즈 뎀, 벗 디 언페이쓰펄 아아 트랩트 바이 이벌 디자여즈.
정직한 자의 공의는 자기를 건지려니와 사악한 자는 자기의 악에 잡히리라

7 Hopes placed in mortals die with them; all the promise of their power comes to nothing.
호웁스 플레이스트 인 모어털즈 다이 윋 뎀 올 더 프라머스 어브 데어 파워 컴즈 투 너씽.
악인은 죽을 때에 그 소망이 끊어지나니 불의의 소망이 없어지느니라

8 The righteous person is rescued from trouble, and it falls on the wicked instead.
더 라이처스 퍼선 이즈 레스큐드 프럼 트러벌, 언드 잇 폴즈 안 더 위커드 인스테드.
의인은 환난에서 구원을 얻으나 악인은 자기의 길로 가느니라

9 With their mouths the godless destroy their neighbors, but through knowledge the righteous escape.
윋 데어 마운즈 더 가들러스 디스트로이 데어 네이버즈, 벗 쓰루 날러지 더 라이처스 이스케입.
악인은 입으로 그의 이웃을 망하게 하여도 의인은 그의 지식으로 말미암아 구원을 얻느니라

10 When the righteous prosper, the city rejoices; when the wicked perish, there are shouts of joy.
웬 더 라이처스 프라스퍼, 더 시티 리조이서즈 웬 더 위커드 페어리쉬, 데어 아아 샤웃스 어브 조이.
의인이 형통하면 성읍이 즐거워하고 악인이 패망하면 기뻐 외치느니라

11 Through the blessing of the upright a city is exalted, but by the mouth of the wicked it is destroyed.
쓰루 더 블레싱 어브 디 업라이트 어 시티 이즈 이그졸티드, 벗 바이 더 마우쓰 어브 더 위커드 잇 이즈 디스트로이드.
성읍은 정직한 자의 축복으로 인하여 진흥하고 악한 자의 입으로 말미암아 무너지느니라

12 Whoever derides their neighbor has no sense, but the one who has understanding holds their tongue.
후에버 디어라이즈 데어 네이버 해즈 노우 센스, 벗 더 원 후 해즈 언더스탠딩 호울즈 데어 텅.
지혜 없는 자는 그의 이웃을 멸시하나 명철한 자는 잠잠하느니라

13 A gossip betrays a confidence, but a trustworthy person keeps a secret.
어 가섭 빗레이즈 어 칸퍼덴스, 벗 어 트러스트워디 퍼선 킵스 어 시크럿.
두루 다니며 한담하는 자는 남의 비밀을 누설하나 마음이 신실한 자는 그런 것을 숨기느니라

14 For lack of guidance a nation falls, but victory is won through many advisers.
포어 랙 어브 가이던스 어 네이션 폴즈, 벗 빅터어리 이즈 원 쓰루 메니 애드바이저즈.
지략이 없으면 백성이 망하여도 지략이 많으면 평안을 누리느니라

15 Whoever puts up security for a stranger will surely suffer, but whoever refuses to shake hands in pledge is safe.
후에버 풋스 업 시큐러티 포어 어 스트레인저 윌 슈얼리 서퍼, 벗 후에버 리퓨지즈 투 셰익 핸즈 인 플레지 이즈 세이프.
타인을 위하여 보증이 되는 자는 손해를 당하여도 보증이 되기를 싫어하는 자는 평안하니라

16 A kindhearted woman gains honor, but ruthless men gain only wealth.
어 킨드하아티드 워먼 게인즈 아너, 벗 루쓸러스 멘 게인 오운리 웰쓰.
유덕한 여자는 존영을 얻고 근면한 남자는 재물을 얻느니라

17 Those who are kind benefit themselves, but the cruel bring ruin on themselves.
도우즈 후 아아 카인드 베너핏 뎀셀브즈, 벗 더 크루얼 브링 루언 안 뎀셀브즈.
인자한 자는 자기의 영혼을 이롭게 하고 잔인한 자는 자기의 몸을 해롭게 하느니라

18 A wicked person earns deceptive wages, but the one who sows righteousness reaps a sure reward.
어 위커드 퍼선 어느즈 디셉티브 웨이저즈, 벗 더 원 후 소우즈 라이처스너스 립스 어 슈어 리워어드.
악인의 삯은 허무하되 공의를 뿌린 자의 상은 확실하니라

19 Truly the righteous attains life, but whoever pursues evil finds death.
트룰리 더 라이처스 어테인즈 라이프, 벗 후에버 퍼수즈 이블 파인즈 데쓰.
공의를 굳게 지키는 자는 생명에 이르고 악을 따르는 자는 사망에 이르느니라

20 The LORD detests those whose hearts are perverse, but he delights in those whose ways are blameless.
더 로어드 디테스트스 도우즈 후즈 하아트스 아아 퍼버스, 벗 히 딜랏스 인 도우즈 후즈 웨이즈 아아 블레임러스.
마음이 굽은 자는 여호와께 미움을 받아도 행위가 온전한 자는 그의 기뻐하심을 받느니라

21 Be sure of this: The wicked will not go unpunished, but those who are righteous will go free.
비 슈어 어브 디스 더 위커드 윌 낫 고우 언퍼니쉬트, 벗 도우즈 후 아아 라이처스 윌 고우 프리.
악인은 피차 손을 잡을지라도 벌을 면하지 못할 것이나 의인의 자손은 구원을 얻으리라

22 Like a gold ring in a pig's snout is a beautiful woman who shows no discretion.
라익 어 고울드 링 인 어 피그즈 스나우트 이즈 어 뷰터펄 워먼 후 쇼우즈 노우 디스크레션.
아름다운 여인이 삼가지 아니하는 것은 마치 돼지 코에 금 고리 같으니라

23 The desire of the righteous ends only in good, but the hope of the wicked only in wrath.
더 디자여 어브 더 라이처스 엔즈 오운리 인 구드, 벗 더 호웊 어브 더 위커드 오운리 인 래쓰.
의인의 소원은 오직 선하나 악인의 소망은 진노를 이루느니라

24 One person gives freely, yet gains even more; another withholds unduly, but comes to poverty.
원 퍼선 기브즈 프릴리, 옛 게인즈 이빈 모어 어너더 위쓰호울즈 언둘리, 벗 컴즈 투 파버티.
흩어 구제하여도 더욱 부하게 되는 일이 있나니 과도히 아껴도 가난하게 될 뿐이니라

25 A generous person will prosper; whoever refreshes others will be refreshed.
어 제너러스 퍼선 윌 프라스퍼 후에버 리프레쉬즈 어더즈 윌 비 리프레쉬트.
구제를 좋아하는 자는 풍족하여질 것이요 남을 윤택하게 하는 자는 자기도 윤택하여지리라

26 People curse the one who hoards grain, but they pray God's blessing on the one who is willing to sell.
피펄 커스 더 원 후 호어즈 그레인, 벗 데이 프레이 가즈 블레싱 안 더 원 후 이즈 윌링 투 셀.
곡식을 내놓지 아니하는 자는 백성에게 저주를 받을 것이나 파는 자는 그의 머리에 복이 임하리라

27 Whoever seeks good finds favor, but evil comes to one who searches for it.
후에버 식스 구드 파인즈 페이버, 벗 이블 컴즈 투 원 후 서치즈 포어 잇.
선을 간절히 구하는 자는 은총을 얻으려니와 악을 더듬어 찾는 자에게는 악이 임하리라

28 Those who trust in their riches will fall, but the righteous will thrive like a green leaf.
도우즈 후 트러스트 인 데어 리처즈 윌 폴, 벗 더 라이처스 윌 쓰라이브 라익 어 그린 리프.
자기의 재물을 의지하는 자는 패망하려니와 의인은 푸른 잎사귀 같아서 번성하리라

29 Whoever brings ruin on their family will inherit only wind, and the fool will be servant to the wise.
후에버 브링즈 루언 안 데어 패멀리 윌 인헤럿 오운리 윈드, 언드 더 풀 윌 비 서번트 투 더 와이즈.
자기 집을 해롭게 하는 자의 소득은 바람이라 미련한 자는 마음이 지혜로운 자의 종이 되리라

30 The fruit of the righteous is a tree of life, and the one who is wise saves lives.
더 프룻 어브 더 라이처스 이즈 어 트리 어브 라이프, 언드 더 원 후 이즈 와이즈 세이브즈 라이브즈.
의인의 열매는 생명 나무라 지혜로운 자는 사람을 얻느니라

31 If the righteous receive their due on earth, how much more the ungodly and the sinner!
이프 더 라이처스 러시브 데어 듀 안 어쓰, 하우 머치 모어 디 언고들리 언드 더 시너!
보라 의인이라도 이 세상에서 보응을 받겠거든 하물며 악인과 죄인이리요

dishonest [disάnist] a. 부정직한	place [pleis] n. 장소, 곳	duplicity [dju:plísəti] n. 불성실
scale [skeil] n. 눈금, 저울눈	promise [prάmis] n. 약속, 계약	shout [ʃaut] vi. 큰소리를 내다
weight [weit] n. 무게, 중량	power [páuər] n. 힘, 능력	gossip [gάsip] n. 잡담, 한담
find [faind] vt. 찾아내다	righteous [ráitʃəs] a. 올바른	refresh [rifréʃ] vt. 기운나게 하다
favor [féivər] n. 호의, 친절	person [pə́:rsən] n. 사람	deceptive [diséptiv] a. 현혹시키는
pride [praid] n. 자랑, 자존심	rescue [réskju:] vt. 구조하다	wage [weidʒ] n. 임금, 급료
disgrace [disgréis] n. 창피, 불명예	trouble [trʌ́bəl] n. 고생, 근심	pursue [pərsú:] vt. 뒤쫓다
humility [hju:míləti] n. 겸손, 겸양	fall [fɔ:l] vi. 떨어지다	wrath [ræθ] n. 격노, 분노

12장 1 Whoever loves discipline loves knowledge, but whoever hates correction is stupid.
후에버 러브즈 디서플런 러브즈 날러지, 벗 후에버 헤잇스 커렉션 이즈 스투퍼드.
훈계를 좋아하는 자는 지식을 좋아하거니와 징계를 싫어하는 자는 짐승과 같으니라

2 Good people obtain favor from the LORD, but he condemns those who devise wicked schemes.
구드 피펄 어브테인 페이버 프럼 더 로어드, 벗 히 컨뎀즈 도우즈 후 디바이즈 위커드 스킴즈.
선인은 여호와께 은총을 받으려니와 악을 꾀하는 자는 정죄하심을 받으리라

3 No one can be established through wickedness, but the righteous cannot be uprooted.
노우 원 캔 비 이스태블리쉬트 쓰루 위커드너스, 벗 더 라이처스 캐낫 비 업루티드.
사람이 악으로서 굳게 서지 못하거니와 의인의 뿌리는 움직이지 아니하느니라

4 A wife of noble character is her husband's crown, but a disgraceful wife is like decay in his bones.
어 와이프 어브 노우벌 케릭터 이즈 허 허즈번즈 크라운, 벗 어 디스그레이스펄 와이프 이즈 라익 디케이 인 히즈 보운즈.
어진 여인은 그 지아비의 면류관이나 욕을 끼치는 여인은 그 지아비의 뼈가 썩음 같게 하느니라

5 The plans of the righteous are just, but the advice of the wicked is deceitful.
더 플랜즈 어브 더 라이처스 아아 저스트, 벗 디 애드바이스 어브 더 위커드 이즈 디싯펄.
의인의 생각은 정직하여도 악인의 도모는 속임이니라

6 The words of the wicked lie in wait for blood, but the speech of the upright rescues them.
더 워즈 어브 더 위커드 라이 인 웨잇 포어 블러드, 벗 더 스피치 어브 디 업라이트 레스큐즈 뎀.
악인의 말은 사람을 엿보아 피를 흘리자 하는 것이거니와 정직한 자의 입은 사람을 구원하느니라

7 The wicked are overthrown and are no more, but the house of the righteous stands firm.
더 위커드 아아 오우버쓰로운 언드 아아 노우 모어, 벗 더 하우스 어브 더 라이처스 스탠즈 펌.
악인은 엎드러져서 소멸되려니와 의인의 집은 서 있으리라

8 A person is praised according to their prudence, and one with a warped mind is despised.
어 퍼선 이즈 프레이즈드 어코어딩 투 데어 프루던스, 언드 원 윋 어 워어프트 마인드 이즈 디스파이즈드.

사람은 그 지혜대로 칭찬을 받으려니와 마음이 굽은 자는 멸시를 받으리라

9 Better to be a nobody and yet have a servant than pretend to be somebody and have no food.
베터 투 비 어 노우바디 언드 옛 해브 어 서번트 던 프리텐드 투 비 섬바디 언드 해브 노우 푸드.
비천히 여김을 받을지라도 종을 부리는 자는 스스로 높은 체하고도 음식이 핍절한 자보다 나으니라

10 The righteous care for the needs of their animals, but the kindest acts of the wicked are cruel.
더 라이처스 케어 포어 더 니즈 어브 데어 애너멀즈, 벗 더 카인더스트 액트스 어브 더 위커드 아아 크루얼.
의인은 자기의 가축의 생명을 돌보나 악인의 긍휼은 잔인이니라

11 Those who work their land will have abundant food, but those who chase fantasies have no sense.
도우즈 후 웍 데어 랜드 윌 해브 어번던트 푸드, 벗 도우즈 후 체이스 팬터시즈 해브 노우 센스.
자기의 토지를 경작하는 자는 먹을 것이 많거니와 방탕한 것을 따르는 자는 지혜가 없느니라

12 The wicked desire the stronghold of evildoers, but the root of the righteous endures.
더 위커드 디자여 더 스트롱호울드 어브 이벌두어즈, 벗 더 룻 어브 더 라이처스 엔듀즈.
악인은 불의의 이익을 탐하나 의인은 그 뿌리로 말미암아 결실하느니라

13 Evildoers are trapped by their sinful talk, and so the innocent escape trouble.
이벌두어즈 아아 트랩트 바이 데어 신펄 톡, 언드 소우 디 이너선트 이스케입 트러벌.
악인은 입술의 허물로 말미암아 그물에 걸려도 의인은 환난에서 벗어나느니라

14 From the fruit of their lips people are filled with good things, and the work of their hands brings them reward.
프럼 더 프룻 어브 데어 립스 피펄 아아 필드 윋 구드 씽즈, 언드 더 웍 어브 데어 핸즈 브링즈 뎀 리워어드.
사람은 입의 열매로 말미암아 복록에 족하며 그 손이 행하는 대로 자기가 받느니라

15 The way of fools seems right to them, but the wise listen to advice.
더 웨이 어브 풀즈 심즈 라이트 투 뎀, 벗 더 와이즈 리선 투 애드바이스.
미련한 자는 자기 행위를 바른 줄로 여기나 지혜로운 자는 권고를 듣느니라

16 Fools show their annoyance at once, but the prudent overlook an insult.
풀즈 쇼우 데어 어노이언스 앳 원스, 벗 더 프루던트 오우벌룩 앤 인설트.
미련한 자는 당장 분노를 나타내거니와 슬기로운 자는 수욕을 참느니라

17 An honest witness tells the truth, but a false witness tells lies.
앤 아너스트 윗너스 텔즈 더 트루쓰, 벗 어 폴스 윗너스 텔즈 라이즈.
진리를 말하는 자는 의를 나타내어도 거짓 증인은 속이는 말을 하느니라

18 The words of the reckless pierce like swords, but the tongue of the wise brings healing.
더 워즈 어브 더 레클러스 피어스 라익 소어즈, 벗 더 텅 어브 더 와이즈 브링즈 힐링.
칼로 찌름 같이 함부로 말하는 자가 있거니와 지혜로운 자의 혀는 양약과 같으니라

19 Truthful lips endure forever, but a lying tongue lasts only a moment.
트루쓰펄 립스 엔듀 퍼레버, 벗 어 라이잉 텅 래스트스 오운리 어 모우먼트.
진실한 입술은 영원히 보존되거니와 거짓 혀는 잠시 동안만 있을 뿐이니라

20 Deceit is in the hearts of those who plot evil, but those who promote peace have joy.
디싯 이즈 인 더 하아트스 어브 도우즈 후 플랏 이벌, 벗 도우즈 후 프러모우트 피스 해브 조이.
악을 꾀하는 자의 마음에는 속임이 있고 화평을 의논하는 자에게는 희락이 있느니라

21 No harm overtakes the righteous, but the wicked have their fill of trouble.
노우 함 오우버테익스 더 라이처스, 벗 더 위커드 해브 데어 필 어브 트러벌.
의인에게는 어떤 재앙도 임하지 아니하려니와 악인에게는 앙화가 가득하리라

22 The LORD detests lying lips, but he delights in people who are trustworthy.
더 로어드 디테스트스 라이잉 립스, 벗 히 딜랏스 인 피펄 후 아아 트러스트워디.
거짓 입술은 여호와께 미움을 받아도 진실하게 행하는 자는 그의 기뻐하심을 받느니라

23 The prudent keep their knowledge to themselves, but a fool's heart blurts out folly.
더 프루던트 킵 데어 날러지 투 뎀셀브즈, 벗 어 풀즈 하아트 블러트스 아웃 팔리.
슬기로운 자는 지식을 감추어도 미련한 자의 마음은 미련한 것을 전파하느니라

24 Diligent hands will rule, but laziness ends in forced labor.
딜리전트 핸즈 윌 룰, 벗 레이지너스 엔즈 인 포어스트 레이버.
부지런한 자의 손은 사람을 다스리게 되어도 게으른 자는 부림을 받느니라

25 Anxiety weighs down the heart, but a kind word cheers it up.
앵자이어티 웨이즈 다운 더 하아트, 벗 어 카인드 워드 치어즈 잇 업.
근심이 사람의 마음에 있으면 그것으로 번뇌하게 되나 선한 말은 그것을 즐겁게 하느니라

26 The righteous choose their friends carefully, but the way of the wicked leads them astray.
더 라이처스 추즈 데어 프렌즈 케어펄리, 벗 더 웨이 어브 더 위커드 리즈 뎀 어스트레이.
의인은 그 이웃의 인도자가 되나 악인의 소행은 자신을 미혹하느니라

27 The lazy do not roast any game, but the diligent feed on the riches of the hunt.
더 레이지 두 낫 로우스트 에니 게임, 벗 더 딜리전트 피드 안 더 리처즈 어브 더 헌트.
게으른 자는 그 잡을 것도 사냥하지 아니하나니 사람의 부귀는 부지런한 것이니라

28 In the way of righteousness there is life; along that path is immortality.
인 더 웨이 어브 라이처스너스 데어 이즈 라이프 얼롱 댓 패쓰 이즈 이모어탤리티.
공의로운 길에 생명이 있나니 그 길에는 사망이 없느니라

stupid [stjú:pid] a. 어리석은	decay [dikéi] vi. 썩다, 부패하다	lip [lip] n. 입술
obtain [əbtéin] vt. 획득하다	deceitful [disí:tfəl] a. 거짓의	annoyance [ənɔ́iəns] n. 성가심
condemn [kəndém] vt. 비난하다	plan [plæn] n. 계획	deceit [disí:t] n. 속임, 사기
through [θru:] prep. …을 통하여	advice [ædváis] n. 충고, 조언	blurt [blə:rt] vt. 누설하다
character [kæriktər] n. 특성	stand [stænd] vi. 서다	labor [léibər] n. 노동, 근로
husband [hʌ́zbənd] n. 남편	praise [preiz] n. 칭찬, 찬양	anxiety [æŋzáiəti] n. 걱정, 근심
crown [kraun] n. 왕관	abundant [əbʌ́ndənt] a. 풍부한	immortality [imɔ:rtæləti] n. 불멸
wife [waif] n. 아내	endure [endjúər] vt. 견디다	force [fɔ:rs] n. 힘, 세력

13장 1 A wise son heeds his father's instruction, but a mocker does not respond to rebukes.
어 와이즈 선 히즈 히즈 파더즈 인스트럭션, 벗 어 마커 더즈 낫 리스판드 투 리븍스.
지혜로운 아들은 아비의 훈계를 들으나 거만한 자는 꾸지람을 즐겨 듣지 아니하느니라

2 From the fruit of their lips people enjoy good things, but the unfaithful have an appetite for violence.
프럼 더 프룻 어브 데어 립스 피펄 엔조이 구드 씽즈, 벗 디 언페이쓰펄 해브 앤 애퍼타이트 포어 바이얼런스.

사람은 입의 열매로 인하여 복록을 누리거니와 마음이 궤사한 자는 강포를 당하느니라

3 Those who guard their lips preserve their lives, but those who speak rashly will come to ruin.
도우즈 후 가아드 데어 립스 프리저브 데어 라이브즈, 벗 도우즈 후 스픽 래슬리 윌 컴 투 루언.
입을 지키는 자는 자기의 생명을 보전하나 입술을 크게 벌리는 자에게는 멸망이 오느니라

4 A sluggard's appetite is never filled, but the desires of the diligent are fully satisfied.
어 슬러거즈 애퍼타이트 이즈 네버 필드, 벗 더 디자여즈 어브 더 딜리전트 아아 풀리 새터스파이드.
게으른 자는 마음으로 원하여도 얻지 못하나 부지런한 자의 마음은 풍족함을 얻느니라

5 The righteous hate what is false, but the wicked make themselves a stench and bring shame on themselves.
더 라이처스 헤이트 웟 이즈 폴스, 벗 더 위커드 메익 뎀셀브즈 어 스텐치 언드 브링 셰임 안 뎀셀브즈.
의인은 거짓말을 미워하나 악인은 행위가 흉악하여 부끄러운 데에 이르느니라

6 Righteousness guards the person of integrity, but wickedness overthrows the sinner.
라이처스너스 가아즈 더 퍼선 어브 인테그러티, 벗 위커드너스 오우버쓰로우즈 더 시너.
공의는 행실이 정직한 자를 보호하고 악은 죄인을 패망하게 하느니라

7 One person pretends to be rich, yet has nothing; another pretends to be poor, yet has great wealth.
원 퍼선 프리텐즈 투 비 리치, 옛 해즈 너씽 어너더 프리텐즈 투 비 푸어, 옛 해즈 그레이트 웰쓰.
스스로 부한 체하여도 아무 것도 없는 자가 있고 스스로 가난한 체하여도 재물이 많은 자가 있느니라

8 A person's riches may ransom their life, but the poor cannot respond to threatening rebukes.
어 퍼선즈 리처즈 메이 랜섬 데어 라이프, 벗 더 푸어 캐낫 리스판드 투 쓰레터닝 리뷰스.
사람의 재물이 자기 생명의 속전일 수 있으나 가난한 자는 협박을 받을 일이 없느니라

9 The light of the righteous shines brightly, but the lamp of the wicked is snuffed out.
더 라이트 어브 더 라이처스 샤인즈 브라잇리, 벗 더 램프 어브 더 위커드 이즈 스너프트 아웃.
의인의 빛은 환하게 빛나고 악인의 등불은 꺼지느니라

10 Where there is strife, there is pride, but wisdom is found in those who take advice.
웨어 데어 이즈 스트라이프, 데어 이즈 프라이드, 벗 위즈덤 이즈 파운드 인 도우즈 후 테익 애드바이스.
교만에서는 다툼만 일어날 뿐이라 권면을 듣는 자는 지혜가 있느니라

11 Dishonest money dwindles away, but whoever gathers money little by little makes it grow.
디사너스트 머니 뒨덜즈 어웨이, 벗 후에버 개더즈 머니 리털 바이 리털 메익스 잇 그로우.
망령되이 얻은 재물은 줄어가고 손으로 모은 것은 늘어가느니라

12 Hope deferred makes the heart sick, but a longing fulfilled is a tree of life.
호웁 디퍼드 메익스 더 하아트 식, 벗 어 롱잉 풀필드 이즈 어 트리 어브 라이프.
소망이 더디 이루어지면 그것이 마음을 상하게 하거니와 소원이 이루어지는 것은 곧 생명 나무니라

13 Whoever scorns instruction will pay for it, but whoever respects a command is rewarded.
후에버 스콘즈 인스트럭션 윌 페이 포어 잇, 벗 후에버 리스펙트스 어 커맨드 이즈 리워어디드.
말씀을 멸시하는 자는 자기에게 패망을 이루고 계명을 두려워하는 자는 상을 받느니라

14 The teaching of the wise is a fountain of life, turning a person from the snares of death.
더 티칭 어브 더 와이즈 이즈 어 파운턴 어브 라이프, 터닝 어 퍼선 프럼 더 스네어즈 어브 데쓰.
지혜 있는 자의 교훈은 생명의 샘이니 사망의 그물에서 벗어나게 하느니라

15 Good judgment wins favor, but the way of the unfaithful leads to their destruction.
구드 저지먼트 윈즈 페이버, 벗 더 웨이 어브 디 언페이쓰펄 리즈 투 데어 디스트럭션.
선한 지혜는 은혜를 베푸나 사악한 자의 길은 험하니라

16 All who are prudent act with knowledge, but fools expose their folly.
올 후 아아 프루던트 액트 윋 날러지, 벗 풀즈 익스포우즈 데어 팔리.
무릇 슬기로운 자는 지식으로 행하거니와 미련한 자는 자기의 미련한 것을 나타내느니라

17 A wicked messenger falls into trouble, but a trustworthy envoy brings healing.
어 위커드 메선저 폴즈 인투 트러벌, 벗 어 트러스트워디 엔보이 브링즈 힐링.
악한 사자는 재앙에 빠져도 충성된 사신은 양약이 되느니라

18 Whoever disregards discipline comes to poverty and shame, but whoever heeds correction is honored.
후 에버 디스리가아즈 디서플런 컴즈 투 파버티 언드 셰임, 벗 후에버 히즈 커렉션 이즈 아너드.
훈계를 저버리는 자에게는 궁핍과 수욕이 이르거니와 경계를 받는 자는 존영을 받느니라

19 A longing fulfilled is sweet to the soul, but fools detest turning from evil.
어 롱잉 풀필드 이즈 스윗 투 더 소울, 벗 풀즈 디테스트 터닝 프럼 이벌.
소원을 성취하면 마음에 달아도 미련한 자는 악에서 떠나기를 싫어하느니라

20 Walk with the wise and become wise, for a companion of fools suffers harm.
웍 윋 더 와이즈 언드 비컴 와이즈, 포어 어 컴패년 어브 풀즈 서퍼즈 함.
지혜로운 자와 동행하면 지혜를 얻고 미련한 자와 사귀면 해를 받느니라

21 Trouble pursues the sinner, but the righteous are rewarded with good things.
트러벌 퍼수즈 더 시너, 벗 더 라이처스 아아 리워어디드 윋 구드 씽즈.
재앙은 죄인을 따르고 선한 보응은 의인에게 이르느니라

22 A good person leaves an inheritance for their children's children, but a sinner's wealth is stored up for the righteous.
어 구드 퍼선 리브즈 앤 인헤러턴스 포어 데어 칠드런즈 칠드런, 벗 어 시너즈 웰쓰 이즈 스토어드 업 포어 더 라이처스.
선인은 그 산업을 자자 손손에게 끼쳐도 죄인의 재물은 의인을 위하여 쌓이느니라

23 An unplowed field produces food for the poor, but injustice sweeps it away.
앤 언플라우드 필드 프러두서즈 푸드 포어 더 푸어, 벗 인저스티스 스윕스 잇 어웨이.
가난한 자는 밭을 경작함으로 양식이 많아지거니와 불의로 말미암아 가산을 탕진하는 자가 있느니라

24 Whoever spares the rod hates their children, but the one who loves their children is careful to discipline them.
후에버 스페어즈 더 라드 헤잇스 데어 칠드런, 벗 더 원 후 러브즈 데어 칠드런 이즈 케어펄 투 디서플런 뎀.
매를 아끼는 자는 그의 자식을 미워함이라 자식을 사랑하는 자는 근실히 징계하느니라

25 The righteous eat to their hearts' content, but the stomach of the wicked goes hungry.
더 라이처스 잇 투 데어 하아트스 칸텐트, 벗 더 스터먹 어브 더 위커드 고우즈 헝그리.
의인은 포식하여도 악인의 배는 주리느니라

heed [hiːd] vt. 주의하다	stench [stentʃ] n. 악취	snuff [snʌf] n. 하찮은 것
fruit [fruːt] n. 과일, 실과	sinner [sínər] n. 죄인	strife [straif] n. 투쟁, 다툼
people [píːpl] n. 사람들	pretend [priténd] vt. …인 체하다	gather [gǽðər] vt. 모으다
appetite [ǽpitàit] n. 식욕, 욕구	rich [ritʃ] a. 부자의, 부유한	sick [sik] a. 병의, 병에 걸린
rash [ræʃ] a. 분별없는, 경솔한	ransom [rǽnsəm] n. 속전	respect [rispékt] n. 존경, 경의
fully [fúli] ad. 충분히, 완전히	threaten [θrétn] vt. 협박하다	expose [ikspóuz] vt. 폭로하다
satisfied [sǽtisfàid] a. 만족한	respond [rispɑ́nd] vi. 응답하다	envoy [énvɔi] n. 사절, 특사
false [fɔːls] a. 그릇된, 틀린	lamp [læmp] n. 등불, 램프	sweet [swiːt] a. 단, 달콤한

14장 1 The wise woman builds her house, but with her own hands the foolish one tears hers down.
더 와이즈 워먼 빌즈 허 하우스, 벗 윋 허 오운 핸즈 더 풀리쉬 원 티어즈 허즈 다운.
지혜로운 여인은 자기 집을 세우되 미련한 여인은 자기 손으로 그것을 허느니라

2 Whoever fears the LORD walks uprightly, but those who despise him are devious in their ways.
후에버 피어즈 더 로어드 웍스 업라잇리, 벗 도우즈 후 디스파이즈 힘 아아 디비어스 인 데어 웨이즈.
정직하게 행하는 자는 여호와를 경외하여도 패역하게 행하는 자는 여호와를 경멸하느니라

3 A fool's mouth lashes out with pride, but the lips of the wise protect them.
어 풀즈 마우쓰 래쉬즈 아웃 윋 프라이드, 벗 더 립스 어브 더 와이즈 프러텍트 뎀.
미련한 자는 교만하여 입으로 매를 자청하고 지혜로운 자의 입술은 자기를 보전하느니라

4 Where there are no oxen, the manger is empty, but from the strength of an ox come abundant harvests.
웨어 데어 아아 노우 악선, 더 메인저 이즈 엠프티, 벗 프럼 더 스트렝쓰 어브 앤 악스 컴 어번던트 하아버스트스.
소가 없으면 구유는 깨끗하려니와 소의 힘으로 얻는 것이 많으니라

5 An honest witness does not deceive, but a false witness pours out lies.
앤 아너스트 윗너스 더즈 낫 디시브, 벗 어 폴스 윗너스 포어즈 아웃 라이즈.
신실한 증인은 거짓말을 아니하여도 거짓 증인은 거짓말을 뱉느니라

6 The mocker seeks wisdom and finds none, but knowledge comes easily to the discerning.
더 마커 식스 위즈덤 언드 파인즈 넌, 벗 날러지 컴즈 이절리 투 더 디서닝.
거만한 자는 지혜를 구하여도 얻지 못하거니와 명철한 자는 지식 얻기가 쉬우니라

7 Stay away from a fool, for you will not find knowledge on their lips.
스테이 어웨이 프럼 어 풀, 포어 유 윌 낫 파인드 날러지 안 데어 립스.
너는 미련한 자의 앞을 떠나라 그 입술에 지식 있음을 보지 못함이니라

8 The wisdom of the prudent is to give thought to their ways, but the folly of fools is deception.
더 위즈덤 어브 더 프루던트 이즈 투 기브 쏫 투 데어 웨이즈, 벗 더 팔리 어브 풀즈 이즈 디셉션.
슬기로운 자의 지혜는 자기의 길을 아는 것이라도 미련한 자의 어리석음은 속이는 것이니라

9 Fools mock at making amends for sin, but goodwill is found among the upright.
풀즈 막 앳 메이킹 어멘즈 포어신, 벗 구될 이즈 파운드 어멍 디 업라이트.
미련한 자는 죄를 심상히 여겨도 정직한 자 중에는 은혜가 있느니라

10 Each heart knows its own bitterness, and no one else can share its joy.
이치 하아트 노우즈 잇스 오운 비터너스, 언드 노우 원 엘스 캔 셰어 잇스 조이.

마음의 고통은 자기가 알고 마음의 즐거움은 타인이 참여하지 못하느니라

11 The house of the wicked will be destroyed, but the tent of the upright will flourish.
더 하우스 어브 더 위커드 윌 비 디스트로이드, 벗 더 텐트 어브 디 업라이트 윌 플러리쉬.
악한 자의 집은 망하겠고 정직한 자의 장막은 흥하리라

12 There is a way that appears to be right, but in the end it leads to death.
데어 이즈 어 웨이 댓 어피어즈 투 비 라이트, 벗 인 디 엔드 잇 리즈 투 데쓰.
어떤 길은 사람이 보기에 바르나 필경은 사망의 길이니라

13 Even in laughter the heart may ache, and rejoicing may end in grief.
이빈 인 래프터 더 하아트 메이 에잌, 언드 리조이싱 메이 엔드 인 그리프.
웃을 때에도 마음에 슬픔이 있고 즐거움의 끝에도 근심이 있느니라

14 The faithless will be fully repaid for their ways, and the good rewarded for theirs.
더 페이쓸러스 윌 비 풀리 리페이드 포어 데어 웨이즈, 언드 더 구드 리워어디드 포어 데어즈.
마음이 굽은 자는 자기 행위로 보응이 가득하겠고 선한 사람도 자기의 행위로 그러하리라

15 The simple believe anything, but the prudent give thought to their steps.
더 심펄 빌리브 에니씽, 벗 더 프루던트 기브 쏫 투 데어 스텝스.
어리석은 자는 온갖 말을 믿으나 슬기로운 자는 자기의 행동을 삼가느니라

16 The wise fear the LORD and shun evil, but a fool is hotheaded and yet feels secure.
더 와이즈 피어 더 로어드 언드 션 이벌, 벗 어 풀 이즈 핫헤디드 언드 옛 필즈 시큘.
지혜로운 자는 두려워하여 악을 떠나나 어리석은 자는 방자하여 스스로 믿느니라

17 A quick-tempered person does foolish things, and the one who devises evil schemes is hated.
어 퀵템퍼드 퍼선 더즈 풀리쉬 씽즈, 언드 더 원 후 디바이지즈 이벌 스킴즈 이즈 헤이터드.
노하기를 속히 하는 자는 어리석은 일을 행하고 악한 계교를 꾀하는 자는 미움을 받느니라

18 The simple inherit folly, but the prudent are crowned with knowledge.
더 심펄 인헤릿 팔리, 벗 더 프루던트 아아 크라운드 윋 날러지.
어리석은 자는 어리석음으로 기업을 삼아도 슬기로운 자는 지식으로 면류관을 삼느니라

19 Evildoers will bow down in the presence of the good, and the wicked at the gates of the righteous.
이벌두어즈 윌 바우 다운 인 더 프레전스 어브 더 구드, 언드 더 위커드 앳 더 게잇스 어브 더 라이처스.
악인은 선인 앞에 엎드리고 불의한 자는 의인의 문에 엎드리느니라

20 The poor are shunned even by their neighbors, but the rich have many friends.
더 푸어 아아 션드 이빈 바이 데어 네이버즈, 벗 더 리치 해브 메니 프렌즈.
가난한 자는 이웃에게도 미움을 받게 되나 부요한 자는 친구가 많으니라

21 It is a sin to despise one's neighbor, but blessed is the one who is kind to the needy.
잇 이즈 어 신 투 디스파이즈 원즈 네이버, 벗 블레스트 이즈 더 원 후 이즈 카인드 투 더 니디.
이웃을 업신여기는 자는 죄를 범하는 자요 빈곤한 자를 불쌍히 여기는 자는 복이 있는 자니라

22 Do not those who plot evil go astray? But those who plan what is good find love and faithfulness.
두 낫 도우즈 후 플랏 이벌 고우 어스트레이? 벗 도우즈 후 플랜 윗 이즈 구드 파인드 러브 언드 페이쓰펄네스.
악을 도모하는 자는 잘못 가는 것이 아니냐 선을 도모하는 자에게는 인자와 진리가 있으리라

23 All hard work brings a profit, but mere talk leads only to poverty.

올 하아드 웍 브링즈 어 프라핏, 벗 미어 톡 리즈 오운리 투 파버티.
모든 수고에는 이익이 있어도 입술의 말은 궁핍을 이룰 뿐이니라

24 The wealth of the wise is their crown, but the folly of fools yields folly.
더 웰쓰 어브 더 와이즈 이즈 데어 크라운, 벗 더 팔리 어브 풀즈 일즈 팔리.
지혜로운 자의 재물은 그의 면류관이요 미련한 자의 소유는 다만 미련한 것이니라

25 A truthful witness saves lives, but a false witness is deceitful.
어 트루쓰펄 윗너스 세이브즈 라이브즈, 벗 어 폴스 윗너스 이즈 디싯펄.
진실한 증인은 사람의 생명을 구원하여도 거짓말을 뱉는 사람은 속이느니라

26 Whoever fears the LORD has a secure fortress, and for their children it will be a refuge.
후에버 피어즈 더 로어드 해즈 어 시큐 포어트러스, 언드 포어 데어 칠드런 잇 윌 비 어 레퓨지.
여호와를 경외하는 자에게는 견고한 의뢰가 있나니 그 자녀들에게 피난처가 있으리라

27 The fear of the LORD is a fountain of life, turning a person from the snares of death.
더 피어 어브 더 로어드 이즈 어 파운턴 어브 라이프, 터닝 어 퍼선 프럼 더 스네어즈 어브 데쓰.
여호와를 경외하는 것은 생명의 샘이니 사망의 그물에서 벗어나게 하느니라

28 A large population is a king's glory, but without subjects a prince is ruined.
어 라아지 파퓰레이션 이즈 어 킹즈 글로어리, 벗 위다우트 서브직트스 어 프린스 이즈 루언드.
백성이 많은 것은 왕의 영광이요 백성이 적은 것은 주권자의 패망이니라

29 Whoever is patient has great understanding, but one who is quick-tempered displays folly.
후에버 이즈 페이션트 해즈 그레이트 언더스탠딩, 벗 원 후 이즈 퀵템퍼드 디스플레이즈 팔리.
노하기를 더디 하는 자는 크게 명철하여도 마음이 조급한 자는 어리석음을 나타내느니라

30 A heart at peace gives life to the body, but envy rots the bones.
어 하아트 앳 피스 기브즈 라이프 투 더 바디, 벗 엔비 랏스 더 보운즈.
평온한 마음은 육신의 생명이나 시기는 뼈를 썩게 하느니라

31 Whoever oppresses the poor shows contempt for their Maker, but whoever is kind to the needy honors God.
후에버 업레시즈 더 푸어 쇼우즈 컨템프트 포어 데어 메이커, 벗 후에버 이즈 카인드 투 더 니디 아너즈 가드.
가난한 사람을 학대하는 자는 그를 지으신 이를 멸시하는 자요 궁핍한 사람을 불쌍히 여기는 자는 주를 공경하는 자니라

32 When calamity comes, the wicked are brought down, but even in death the righteous seek refuge in God.
웬 컬래머티 컴즈, 더 위커드 아아 브롯 다운, 벗 이빈 인 데쓰 더 라이처스 식 레퓨지 인 가드.
악인은 그의 환난에 엎드러져도 의인은 그의 죽음에도 소망이 있느니라

33 Wisdom reposes in the heart of the discerning and even among fools she lets herself be known.
위즈덤 리포우지즈 인 더 하아트 어브 더 디서닝 언드 이빈 어멍 풀즈 쉬 렛스 허셀프 비 노운.
지혜는 명철한 자의 마음에 머물거니와 미련한 자의 속에 있는 것은 나타나느니라

34 Righteousness exalts a nation, but sin condemns any people.
라이처스너스 이그졸트스 어 네이션, 벗 신 컨뎀즈 에니 피펄.
공의는 나라를 영화롭게 하고 죄는 백성을 욕되게 하느니라

35 A king delights in a wise servant, but a shameful servant arouses his fury.
어 킹 딜랏스 인 어 와이즈 서번트, 벗 어 셰임펄 서번트 어아우지즈 히즈 퓨리.
슬기롭게 행하는 신하는 왕에게 은총을 입고 욕을 끼치는 신하는 그의 진노를 당하느니라

ox [ɔks] n. 황소	amend [əménd] vt. 수정하다	secure [sikjúər] a. 안전한
manger [méindʒər] n. 여물통	goodwill [gúdwíl] n. 호의, 친절	profit [práfit] n. 이익, 수익
empty [émpti] a. 빈, 공허한	each [iːtʃ] a. 각각의	population [pàpjəléiʃən] n. 인구
strength [streŋkθ] n. 세기, 힘	share [ʃɛər] n. 몫, 할당	oppress [əprés] vt. 압박하다
witness [wítnis] n. 증언	flourish [flə́ːriʃ] vi. 번성하다	contempt [kəntémpt] n. 경멸, 모욕
pour [pɔːr] vt. 따르다, 쏟다	appear [əpíər] vi. 나타나다	repose [ripóuz] n. 휴식, 휴양
seek [siːk] vt. 찾다, 추구하다	ache [eik] vi. 아프다, 쑤시다	arouse [əráuz] vt. 깨우다
easily [íːzəli] ad. 용이하게	believe [bilíːv] vt. 믿다	mere [miər] a. 단순한

15장 1 A gentle answer turns away wrath, but a harsh word stirs up anger.
어 젠털 앤서 턴즈 어웨이 래쓰, 벗 어 하아쉬 워드 스터즈 업 앵거.
유순한 대답은 분노를 쉬게 하여도 과격한 말은 노를 격동하느니라

2 The tongue of the wise adorns knowledge, but the mouth of the fool gushes folly.
더 텅 어브 더 와이즈 어돈즈 날러지, 벗 더 마우쓰 어브 더 풀 거쉬즈 팔리.
지혜 있는 자의 혀는 지식을 선히 베풀고 미련한 자의 입은 미련한 것을 쏟느니라

3 The eyes of the LORD are everywhere, keeping watch on the wicked and the good.
디 아이즈 어브 더 로어드 아아 에브리웨어, 키핑 와치 안 더 위커드 언드 더 구드.
여호와의 눈은 어디서든지 악인과 선인을 감찰하시느니라

4 The soothing tongue is a tree of life, but a perverse tongue crushes the spirit.
더 수딩 텅 이즈 어 트리 어브 라이프, 벗 어 퍼버스 텅 크러쉬즈 더 스피럿.
온순한 혀는 곧 생명 나무이지만 패역한 혀는 마음을 상하게 하느니라

5 A fool spurns a parent's discipline, but whoever heeds correction shows prudence.
어 풀스 펀즈 어 페런트스 디서플런, 벗 후에버 히즈 커렉션 쇼우즈 프루던스.
아비의 훈계를 업신여기는 자는 미련한 자요 경계를 받는 자는 슬기를 얻을 자니라

6 The house of the righteous contains great treasure, but the income of the wicked brings ruin.
더 하우스 어브 더 라이처스 컨테인즈 그레이트 트레저, 벗 디 인컴 어브 더 위커드 브링즈 루언.
의인의 집에는 많은 보물이 있어도 악인의 소득은 고통이 되느니라

7 The lips of the wise spread knowledge, but the hearts of fools are not upright.
더 립스 어브 더 와이즈 스프레드 날러지, 벗 더 하아트스 어브 풀즈 아아 낫 업라이트.
지혜로운 자의 입술은 지식을 전파하여도 미련한 자의 마음은 정함이 없느니라

8 The LORD detests the sacrifice of the wicked, but the prayer of the upright pleases him.
더 로어드 디테스트스 더 새크러파이스 어브 더 위커드, 벗 더 프레어 어브 디 업라이트 플리지즈 힘.
악인의 제사는 여호와께서 미워하셔도 정직한 자의 기도는 그가 기뻐하시느니라

9 The LORD detests the way of the wicked, but he loves those who pursue righteousness.
더 로어드 디테스트스 더 웨이 어브 더 위커드, 벗 히 러브즈 도우즈 후 퍼수 라이처스너스.
악인의 길은 여호와께서 미워하셔도 공의를 따라가는 자는 그가 사랑하시느니라

10 Stern discipline awaits anyone who leaves the path; the one who hates correction will die.
스턴 디서플런 어웨잇스 에니원 후 리브즈 더 패쓰 더 원 후 헤잇스 커렉션 윌 다이.
도를 배반하는 자는 엄한 징계를 받을 것이요 견책을 싫어하는 자는 죽을 것이니라

11 Death and Destruction lie open before the LORD—how much more do human hearts!
데쓰 언드 디스트럭션 라이 오우펀 비포어 더 로어드 하우 머치 모어 두 휴먼 하아트스!
스올과 아바돈도 여호와의 앞에 드러나거든 하물며 사람의 마음이리요

12 Mockers resent correction, so they avoid the wise.
마커즈 리젠트 커렉션, 소우 데이 어보이드 더 와이즈.
거만한 자는 견책 받기를 좋아하지 아니하며 지혜 있는 자에게로 가지도 아니하느니라

13 A happy heart makes the face cheerful, but heartache crushes the spirit.
어 해피 하아트 메익스 더 페이스 치어펄, 벗 하아테익 크러쉬즈 더 스피릿.
마음의 즐거움은 얼굴을 빛나게 하여도 마음의 근심은 심령을 상하게 하느니라

14 The discerning heart seeks knowledge, but the mouth of a fool feeds on folly.
더 디서닝 하아트 식스 날러지, 벗 더 마우쓰 어브 어 풀 피즈 안 팔리.
명철한 자의 마음은 지식을 요구하고 미련한 자의 입은 미련한 것을 즐기느니라

15 All the days of the oppressed are wretched, but the cheerful heart has a continual feast.
올 더 데이즈 어브 디 업레스트 아아 레치드, 벗 더 치어펄 하아트 해즈 어 컨티뉴얼 피스트.
고난 받는 자는 그 날이 다 험악하나 마음이 즐거운 자는 항상 잔치하느니라

16 Better a little with the fear of the LORD than great wealth with turmoil.
베터 어 리털 윋 더 피어 어브 더 로어드 던 그레이트 웰쓰 윋 터모일.
가산이 적어도 여호와를 경외하는 것이 크게 부하고 번뇌하는 것보다 나으니라

17 Better a small serving of vegetables with love than a fattened calf with hatred.
베터 어 스몰 서빙 어브 베지터벌즈 윋 러브 던 어 패턴드 캐프 윋 헤잇러드.
채소를 먹으며 서로 사랑하는 것이 살진 소를 먹으며 서로 미워하는 것보다 나으니라

18 A hot-tempered person stirs up conflict, but the one who is patient calms a quarrel.
어 핫템퍼드 퍼선 스터즈 업 칸플릭트, 벗 더 원 후 이즈 페이션트 캄즈 어 쿼럴.
분을 쉽게 내는 자는 다툼을 일으켜도 노하기를 더디 하는 자는 시비를 그치게 하느니라

19 The way of the sluggard is blocked with thorns, but the path of the upright is a highway.
더 웨이 어브 더 슬러거드 이즈 블락트 윋 쏜즈, 벗 더 패쓰 어브 디 업라이트 이즈 어 하이웨이.
게으른 자의 길은 가시 울타리 같으나 정직한 자의 길은 대로니라

20 A wise son brings joy to his father, but a foolish man despises his mother.
어 와이즈 선 브링즈 조이 투 히즈 파더, 벗 어 풀리쉬 맨 디스파이지즈 히즈 머더.
지혜로운 아들은 아비를 즐겁게 하여도 미련한 자는 어미를 업신여기느니라

21 Folly brings joy to one who has no sense, but whoever has understanding keeps a straight course.
팔리 브링즈 조이 투 원 후 해즈 노우 센스, 벗 후에버 해즈 언더스탠딩 킵스 어 스트레이트 코어스.
무지한 자는 미련한 것을 즐겨 하여도 명철한 자는 그 길을 바르게 하느니라

22 Plans fail for lack of counsel, but with many advisers they succeed.
플랜즈 페일 포어 랙 어브 카운설, 벗 윋 메니 애드바이저즈 데이 석시드.

의논이 없으면 경영이 무너지고 지략이 많으면 경영이 성립하느니라

23 A person finds joy in giving an apt reply—and how good is a timely word!
어 퍼선 파인즈 조이 인 기빙 앤 앱트 리플라이 언드 하우 구드 이즈 어 타임리 워드!
사람은 그 입의 대답으로 말미암아 기쁨을 얻나니 때에 맞는 말이 얼마나 아름다운고

24 The path of life leads upward for the prudent to keep them from going down to the realm of the dead.
더 패쓰 어브 라이프 리즈 어프워드 포어 더 프루던트 투 킵 뎀 프럼 고우잉 다운 투 더 렐므 어브 더 데드.
지혜로운 자는 위로 향한 생명 길로 말미암음으로 그 아래에 있는 스올을 떠나게 되느니라

25 The LORD tears down the house of the proud, but he sets the widow's boundary stones in place.
더 로어드 티어즈 다운 더 하우스 어브 더 프라우드, 벗 히 셋스 더 위도우즈 바운더리 스토운즈 인 플레이스.
여호와는 교만한 자의 집을 허시며 과부의 지계를 정하시느니라

26 The LORD detests the thoughts of the wicked, but gracious words are pure in his sight.
더 로어드 디테스트스 더 쏫스 어브 더 위커드, 벗 그레이셔스 워즈 아아 퓨 인 히즈 사이트.
악한 꾀는 여호와께서 미워하시나 선한 말은 정결하니라

27 The greedy bring ruin to their households, but the one who hates bribes will live.
더 그리디 브링 루언 투 데어 하우스호울즈, 벗 더 원 후 헤잇스 브라이브즈 윌 리브.
이익을 탐하는 자는 자기 집을 해롭게 하나 뇌물을 싫어하는 자는 살게 되느니라

28 The heart of the righteous weighs its answers, but the mouth of the wicked gushes evil.
더 하아트 어브 더 라이처스 웨이즈 잇스 앤서즈, 벗 더 마우쓰 어브 더 위커드 거쉬즈 이벌.
의인의 마음은 대답할 말을 깊이 생각하여도 악인의 입은 악을 쏟느니라

29 The LORD is far from the wicked, but he hears the prayer of the righteous.
더 로어드 이즈 파아 프럼 더 위커드, 벗 히 히어즈 더 프레어 어브 더 라이처스.
여호와는 악인을 멀리 하시고 의인의 기도를 들으시느니라

30 Light in a messenger's eyes brings joy to the heart, and good news gives health to the bones.
라이트 인 어 메선저즈 아이즈 브링즈 조이 투 더 하아트, 언드 구드 뉴즈 기브즈 헬쓰 투 더 보운즈.
눈이 밝은 것은 마음을 기쁘게 하고 좋은 기별은 뼈를 윤택하게 하느니라

31 Whoever heeds life-giving correction will be at home among the wise.
후에버 히즈 라이프기빙 커렉션 윌 비 앳 호움 어멍 더 와이즈.
생명의 경계를 듣는 귀는 지혜로운 자 가운데에 있느니라

32 Those who disregard discipline despise themselves, but the one who heeds correction gains understanding.
도우즈 후 디스리가아드 디서플런 디스파이즈 뎀셀브즈, 벗 더 원 후 히즈 커렉션 게인즈 언더스탠딩.
훈계 받기를 싫어하는 자는 자기의 영혼을 경히 여김이라 견책을 달게 받는 자는 지식을 얻느니라

33 Wisdom's instruction is to fear the LORD, and humility comes before honor.
위즈덤즈 인스트럭션 이즈 투 피어 더 로어드, 언드 휴밀리티 컴즈 비포어 아너.
여호와를 경외하는 것은 지혜의 훈계라 겸손은 존귀의 길잡이니라

gentle [dʒéntl] a. 온화한	sacrifice [sǽkrəfàis] n. 희생	calm [kɑːm] a. 고요한, 조용한
answer [ǽnsər] n. 대답, 회답	await [əwéit] vt. …을 기다리다	quarrel [kwɔ́ːrəl] n. 싸움, 말다툼
harsh [hɑːrʃ] a. 거친, 껄껄한	destruction [distrʌ́kʃən] n. 파괴	lack [læk] n. 부족
stir [stəːr] vt. 움직이다	resent [rizént] vt. …에 분개하다	counsel [káunsəl] n. 의논, 협의
gush [gʌʃ] n. 용솟음쳐 나옴	spurn [spəːrn] vt. 퇴짜 놓다	reply [riplái] vi. 대답하다
crush [krʌʃ] vt. 짓밟다	wretch [retʃ] n. 가엾은 사람	greedy [gríːdi] a. 욕심 많은
spirit [spírit] n. 정신, 영	turmoil [tə́ːrmɔil] n. 소란, 소동	bribe [braib] n. 뇌물
income [ínkʌm] n. 수입, 소득	vegetable [védʒətəbəl] n. 야채	before [bifɔ́ːr] ad. 앞에

도서출판 사랑의장막 저서들

분별과 투시로 열리는 영적세계
저자 김다윗

우상 숭배와 음란으로 실패하는 삶의 원인을
규명해 주고 승리의 삶으로 이끌어주는 안내서이다.

14차원으로 열리는 성령의 세계 – 제1권 불의 4차원
저자 김다윗

하나님의 자녀로서 권세 있는 삶을 살아가는 비결은 오직 성령의
충만함에 있다. 이 책은 깊은 기도의 영성으로 열리는 성령의
3속성을 14단계로 풀어 쉽게 이해할 수 있도록 설명하고 있다.

사랑하는 사람들을 향한 사랑의 노래
저자 이해경

시집으로 자녀를 향한 사랑의 노래, 남편과 아내를 향한
사랑의 노래, 하나님을 향한 사랑의 노래, 비전을 향한
사랑의 노래가 수록되어 있다.

개역개정 지혜의 성경 잠언 따라쓰기
사랑의장막 편집부

잠언은 우리 자녀들을 명철하며, 지혜롭게,
공의롭게, 정의롭게, 정직하게 자라나게 합니다.

개역개정 약속의 성경 요절 따라쓰기
사랑의장막 편집부

성경은 하나님의 약속으로 가득합니다. 약속의 성경 요절따라쓰기는
우리 자녀들이 예수님을 믿는 믿음 안에서 천국에 대한 확실한 소망을
가지고 살아가기를 바라는 마음으로 만든 책입니다.

NIV개정 지혜의 성경 영어잠언 따라쓰기 1, 2 (전 2권)
사랑의장막 편집부

영어잠언 따라쓰기를 쓰면서 좋은 영어 글씨체를 갖게 되고,
원어민 발음과 한국어 성경(개역개정)을 수록하여 영어 잠언이 쉽게
읽어집니다. 또한 각 페이지마다 숙어와 예문, 각 장마다 단어를 정리하여
영어 해석에 도움이 됩니다.

NIV개정 약속의 성경 영어 요절 따라쓰기
사랑의장막 편집부

성경은 하나님의 약속으로 가득합니다. 약속의 성경 영어요절 따라쓰기는
약속의 성경 요절 따라쓰기를 영어판(NIV개정)으로 만든 것입니다. 하나님
의 약속들을 마음판에 새기며, 천국에 대한 확실한 소망을 가지고 세상에
서 성령의 능력으로 빛과 소금이 되기를 원합니다.